WRITE YOUR MEMOIR

FROM FIRST IDEAS TO FINISHED BOOK

KAY SANGER

PATHMAKER PRESS

Book design by Linda Morehouse, www.WeBuildBooks.com
Illustrations by Tom Sanger

ISBN: 978-0-9891990-0-1

Printed in the United States of America

Published by Pathmaker Press
7514 Girard Ave., Ste. 1325
La Jolla, CA 92037-5199
www.PathmakerPress.com

To Tom and my writing friends,
with deep appreciation for their support.

ACKNOWLEDGMENTS

The idea for this book grew from the experience of teaching writing classes and leading read-and-critique memoir-writing groups for 20 years. It contains suggestions and exercises that I have honed from the feedback of those students. I am grateful for their honesty and ideas. They have taught me far more than I have taught them.

In particular, I want to acknowledge the inspiration and support of the women in my Paper Mates writing group: Gerta Ambrosek, Britta Brice, Beverly Fink, Stephanie Shapiro, Marianne Sipe, Judy Skelton, Marcia Vaicek and Ferne Weiner. I also want to thank author Tom Larson, who first taught me the value and art of writing memoir.

I appreciate the help of the following people who contributed to the creation of this book with their suggestions, proofreading, and technical support: Kristin Barrett, Nancy Denneny, Scott Gordon, Olga Krambs, Joan Mangan, Sylvie Prewo, Carolyn Schadle, Ted Sanger, Mary Ann Schatz, and Pat Vellinga. I especially am grateful to Linda Morehouse of We Build Books, who designed this book with skill and creativity.

My greatest appreciation goes to my husband, Tom Sanger, who has edited my work over the years and remains steadfast as my chief encourager and editor. He also created the book's illustrations. I could not have written this book without him.

TABLE OF CONTENTS

INTRODUCTION

"THE UNEXAMINED LIFE IS NOT WORTH LIVING."
—Socrates. Athens, 399 B.C.

Have you always wanted to write about your life but can't get started? Do you have ideas for your memoir written on scraps of paper that languish in a box somewhere? Would you like to write your story before you're too old to remember the events, but you just don't know where to begin?

This book will help you finally achieve your goal. It will guide you through ten steps to complete a memoir you can proudly share with your family and friends and perhaps sell to a wider audience. I have encouraged many people to write their memoirs by following these steps, even though they had nagging doubts. I know you can do it too. Each chapter will build on the next, giving you examples, tips, worksheets, and exercises to show you the way.

"OK," you may say, "but why should I write a memoir? I'm not famous. I think I've had an interesting life, but who would want to read about it? My own children don't want to take the time to hear my stories."

Many people have doubts like yours. Yet, like all of us who have lived on the planet for a number of decades, you have many fascinating stories to tell. Step 1 will help you clarify your reasons for writing a memoir. It will show you why it is important to write about your life. Your experiences have given you wisdom and insights. Now is the time to share them.

You may be wondering, "What part of my life should I write about?" The answer is, you should write about your most compelling and memorable experiences. You can't write about every event in your life, of course, so you need to select those that are most significant to you. Those stories will interest your readers, too. Step 2 provides a series of exercises to help you decide which life events you want to include in your memoir.

"Where do I begin?" Many people fail to write a memoir because they don't know where to start. The task of writing about a lifetime of experiences seems so daunting. In Step 3 you will plan the scope of your memoir. You will learn how to organize your stories and determine how to add photos and memorabilia. You will create a Memoir Notebook to provide a framework for collecting your stories as you write them scene by scene.

"OK, but I can't remember much about some of my life events!" Yes, you can, if you work at it. Step 4 gives you suggestions for rediscovering those elusive memories through techniques such as visualization, listening to music, perusing old photos, and spontaneous writing. As you try these exercises, you will be amazed at how many long-forgotten memories come back to you. You will learn to use all your senses to recreate scenes from your past.

"But I'm not a very good writer," you say. "I never really learned how." Step 5 will let you in on a secret that all authors know: the way you learn how to write is by writing. It's like any other skill, such as playing tennis or the piano. You can't expect yourself to do well unless you practice. In this step you will find writing exercises to develop your skills and confidence.

Now you protest, "I've never written a whole book before. How do I write a book-long account of my life that people will want to read?" In Step 6, you will learn how to write engaging stories. Exercises in this step will help you set scenes with memorable details and add dramatic action to your stories with conflict and tension.

"What about the people in my stories? How can I make them sound real in my writing? I'm worried I won't write about them accurately and I will hurt people's feelings." In Step 7 you will learn how to recreate dialogue and enliven the people in your stories by showing us their gestures, speech patterns, actions, and motivations. You also will consider how to describe them with honesty and fairness.

"Will writing a memoir give me new insights about my life?" Definitely. When you write about your life, you not only recreate scenes, but you also will reveal how you felt about what occurred. As a result, you will uncover emotional truths and may even discover the arc of your life experiences. Step 8 directs you through writing exercises to consider the meaning of those life experiences.

"Once I've written my stories, where do I go from there?" Step 9 teaches you how to revise your book so it will be ready for others to read. Exercises will help you decide the order of your stories, whether you should include them all, and how to polish your writing for the final book.

"How do I turn my manuscript into a book?" Step 10 provides ideas to help you create the kind book you want. You'll learn about a variety of options for printing and publishing your book, from do-it-yourself desktop publishing to professional printing, from making an online book to finding an agent or a publisher.

The goal of this book is to help you complete a memoir that you can sell or give to your family, friends, or business associates. This book is short, with steps and techniques that are simple to understand. You can find many excellent books filled with useful information about writing a memoir. The "Suggested Readings" section of this book contains a list of good ones that I think you will find helpful. All of them contain useful information, but none spells out the exact process of writing a memoir in ten steps as this book does. *Write Your Memoir* will give you the tools to write your stories and visualize your completed book.

I suggest you buy an inexpensive spiral notebook with lined pages to use for completing the exercises in this book and writing a first draft of your stories by hand. You also may complete some of the exercises directly on the pages of this book.

It is often said that life is a journey, filled with twists and surprises that shape you. The act of writing about your life is also a journey, filled with unexpected insights, growth, and joy. I invite you to begin that journey of exploring your life with this book. Let it be your guide as you write your stories and discover their significance, step by step.

I want to write a memoir about coming of age in the 1960s, with the social changes that happened then - women wanting careers, the Pill, Civil Rights divisions, the Vietnam War.

While I didn't burn my bra or march for big causes, my actions were influenced by the upheaval.

I want my granddaughters to know what it was like for women whose only job choices were nurse, secretary or teacher, and how it felt to be viewed as a sex symbol when we wanted more.

STEP 1

WHY WRITE YOUR MEMOIR?

"ALL WRITERS ARE EMBARKED ON A QUEST OF SOME KIND,
AND YOU'RE ENTITLED TO GO ON YOURS."
—William Zinsser
Writing About Your Life: A Journey into the Past

YOU MAY HAVE WANTED TO WRITE about your life for a long time now. Perhaps an idea has been simmering on the back of your imaginary stove. Every once in a while it bubbles to the surface, but then the fire dies down and you forget about it for a while.

It could be that you have led an exciting life and people have suggested that you should write about it. Or maybe you want to profile your parents and explain to your grandchildren what it was like to grow up with them during the 20th century. Perhaps you want to detail your experiences for a broader audience by writing about how you dealt with chemotherapy. Or you want to chronicle the way you ran a successful company while raising two children as a single parent. You may want to write a memoir just for yourself, to sort out the meaning of your time on Earth.

These are all good reasons to write a memoir. Your ideas may be different from these and equally valid. No matter what your reasons for wanting to write, it's important to understand your motivations. They will provide you with the inspiration you need to finish your book.

A major reason why people fail to write a memoir is because of their fears. They don't believe deep down that their story is important to tell. They don't acknowledge that they are entitled to write about their lives. They are afraid that no one will be interested. They fear that others will question their telling of events. They worry that they won't be able to write about their lives in a compelling way. In so doing, they fail to give themselves the license and the freedom to make their voices heard.

How can you overcome doubts like these? Begin by acknowledging that your life matters and that you have as much right to write about your experiences as anyone else. Give yourself permission to tell how you perceived it all. Write about others in your life with honesty and compassion. Remind yourself constantly that you are entitled to share your truth.

You could argue that you owe it to future generations to tell the story of your life. If you don't, your life will seem as fuzzy to your grandchildren as the lives of your grandparents do to you. Your reactions to the political, financial, and social events of your era may be vital to a reader who is facing similar challenges in the future. You have wisdom to share about your experiences that may help others lead more enlightened and secure lives.

To resonate with your readers, you need to write honestly about your life experiences—the obstacles, the risks, the successes, and the failures. How did you react to what happened to you? How did you try to take charge? What kind of person are you? What can others learn from you?

You may figure that you have told your stories orally and that's good enough. Yet, will others remember? When you tell a story aloud, it's a momentary, fleeting event. When you write it down, the story can be reread and reconsidered.

Like you, perhaps, I spent many hours listening to my parents' stories around the dinner table. They told about how they met, how they managed during the rationing of World War II, how they made some of their dreams come true, and how they failed at others. And although I heard these same stories over and over, I don't remember many of the details now that my parents are gone. How I wish one of them had written it all down.

Writing about your life allows you to uncover the patterns of your seemingly random experiences. It gives you the opportunity to relive parts of your life and to finally understand what happened. By writing down these stories, you gain insights into your actions and see their significance. When you frame the moments of your life into a narrative, their meaning will come into focus. Out of the dimness of memory will come new visions, new reflections, and new understandings.

Your memoir will be a gift to future generations, possibly more important than property or possessions. Give yourself permission to write it now.

Reasons to Write a Memoir

⤜⊚⤝

For Your Family

Your memoir will enrich the lives of your family by bringing to life past events that otherwise would be lost. You can become the family historian who will tell your children, nieces, and nephews about the exploits, drama, and achievements of older family members, including yourself. Your heirs will want to know about your life someday, even if they don't seem interested right now.

Wouldn't you love to know what your grandparents thought about? How they dealt with lack of money, young love, raising so many children, and death? They look serious and inscrutable in those old photos. Even if they are smiling, you wonder what was behind that façade in front of the camera. Likewise, your grandchildren or interested readers will want to know what you thought about as you negotiated life's obstacles.

⤜⊚⤝

To Keep Alive the Memory of a Relative and Pass along Family Traditions

You may be the only person alive who still knows the old family stories about your parents, grandparents, or other relatives. Perhaps you can tell funny and poignant stories about large gatherings for Thanksgivings when everyone cooked a special dish, or neighborhood Fourth of July parades, or family reunions with your cousins every summer. Your writing about these people and events may be the only way the next generation knows about them.

❧

To Understand Your Own Life

When you write a narrative of your life, you begin to see its meaning. You glimpse the arc of your life journey. You come to terms with the way you handled the challenges that stood in your way. Our lives are messy and busy. We seldom have time to think about the significance of it all. Yet the human need to understand the meaning of our lives is powerful.

When you write about your experiences and your emotional reactions, you release pent-up tensions. Whether you are writing to recount joyous experiences or to unburden yourself from the weight of an untold story, the act of writing about it will give you new understandings. It will allow you to celebrate the distance you've traveled and to reflect on the achievements that have brought you to the place where you reside today.

༺⟋⟍༻

To Organize Your Photos

Perhaps it's finally time to tackle those boxes stuffed with old photos. If you don't, no one else will. Thirty years from now, no one will be able to identify the people, places, or significance of those pictures.

If you haven't already, start this organizational project now. It may take you several months. Go through all your photos and organize them by year or theme. Keep only the best ones and write brief captions about them, identifying the people and events you recognize. With these photos you have the opportunity to create an illustrated memoir that will be an historical treasure.

༺⟋⟍༻

To Write About a Specific Subject

Maybe you want to write a memoir about overcoming breast cancer, or raising a deaf child, or your trips to China over the last thirty years. Your topic may interest many people outside of your family.

Write down your personal stories about the subject. Tell how you felt and what you learned. Think about publishing your book to share your experiences and insights with others.

ᒕᘐᕲᘒᕬ

To Leave to an Historical Society or a Professional Organization

Write about a topic you have researched and studied. Then instead of publishing it as a business or academic text, personalize your subject by placing yourself in the middle of it. Make the information livelier by showing how you experienced the research, how you reached your conclusions, and what you personally learned. You may be able to sell your book to a wide audience. You also could donate it to a university, museum, or archive.

EXERCISE
WHO WILL READ IT?

Make a list of the people you think could be the audience for your book. Picture them in your mind and then write a few paragraphs about why you want to tell them your story. What are the important events or insights that you would like to pass along to these readers?

WORKSHEET

WHY DO I WANT TO WRITE A MEMOIR?

There are many reasons why people write about their lives. Look over the list below. Star the reasons that are similar to yours and write notes next to those reasons. You may want to add your own reasons to this list. Summarize your thoughts below or use a spiral-bound writing notebook for all your exercises.

❑ <u>For my family</u>
What do I want them to know about me?

_____

_____

_____

_____

❑ <u>To keep alive the memory of relatives or friends</u>
Whom do I want to write about?

_____

_____

_____

❑ <u>For myself</u>
What do I want to understand and appreciate?

_____

_____

_____

❑ <u>To organize my photos</u>
What slice of my life do I want to write about
and illustrate?

_____

_____

_____

_____

❑ <u>To write about a specific subject</u>
Travels? Illness? Raising a child?

_____

_____

_____

_____

❑ <u>To leave to a historical society for my town</u>
<u>or a professional organization.</u>

_____

_____

_____

_____

Why do *you* want to write your memoir?

_____

_____

_____

_____

_____

_____

_____

What is Stopping You?

Now that you have identified some of the reasons why you want to write your memoir, it's time to deal with the elephant in the room: What is stopping you?

Somewhere in the back of your mind you may have nagging doubts. *Who would read it? Who cares about my life? I've never written a book before. What makes me think I can do it now? Maybe I will offend a family member?*

You aren't alone in having these doubts. Everyone has them. But you can't let them squash your memoir-writing project. Not if you really want to write your life story. You need to respond to that pesky inner critic who whispers those doubts in your ear.

My inner critic looks something like that troll in the Norwegian folk tale about the Three Billy Goats Gruff. In that familiar story, the troll sits under a bridge and threatens to gobble up anyone who tries to cross over to feast on the greener pastures beyond.

My critical troll threatens to stop me from writing authentic scenes by reminding me of all the reasons why I can't or shouldn't do it. He points out how upset my sister might be with me if I told THAT story. He questions my nerve to write honestly about our father. He wonders if I rationally could handle the delicate topic of sibling jealousy.

Like the biggest Billy Goat Gruff, I need to knock that critical troll off the bridge and then stroll confidently across to achieve my goal.

Yet all of us know that pushing away a personal critic isn't easy. I've seen people sabotage their memoirs before they even begin, because they worry about how others will react to what they write. By so doing, they assign more importance and value to others than to themselves.

If you want to write your memoir, now is the time to resolve your concerns.

WORKSHEET

WHAT CONCERNS DO I HAVE ABOUT WRITING MY MEMOIR?

Listed below are some of the common worries that plague memoir writers. Look them over. Do any of them speak for you? Check the items that sound like what your inner critic says to you and write a note about it in the margin. You also may want to add your own specific concerns to this list.

❑ Others may not find my life interesting. I just did what was expected of me at the time.

❑ I think my life was fascinating, but who would read it? Some people say I should write a book about my experiences, but I worry that no one would be interested.

❑ My kids aren't interested in my stories. They listen half-heartedly when I tell them about past events. So why should I write about these events?

❑ I'm not a very good writer. How can I write about my life so that it would be interesting to someone else?

❑ I don't know where to begin to organize my life story. Should I start at my birth? How do I decide what to put in and leave out of my story? How should I end it?

❑ What will other people think of me? Will they think I am bragging if I write about my accomplishments? Maybe I should just create scrapbooks with photos.

❑ I might hurt _____'s feelings if I really tell the truth. That could upset the family or ruin a friendship. It might dig up old resentments.

❑ This is just too painful. I've buried it for so long. What will happen if I dredge it all up again? Will I go into a depression?

What concerns do *you* have about writing your memoir?

_____

_____

_____

_____

_____

_____

EXERCISE

WHAT COULD SABOTAGE MY MEMOIR?

Now it's time to acknowledge each of these concerns and determine a way to overcome them so you can complete your memoir. Most people who write about their lives share some of these worries.

Choose one concern you identified from the worksheet. On a page in your spiral-bound writing notebook, write the concern as a title at the top of the page, and then write for ten minutes about it. Set a timer. Write anything that comes to your mind.

SUMMARY EXERCISE

WHY I WANT TO WRITE MY MEMOIR

In your spiral-bound writing notebook, write at least one page about why you want to write your memoir. Be specific. What do you hope to accomplish by writing your story? Include the concerns that could derail your project and state how you will work around those. Put your pen on the paper and don't stop until you have said all you want to say about why you want to write this memoir.

TIPS

❏   Purchase an inexpensive lined spiral-bound notebook to use for writing practice in each of the ten steps. Use it for your first drafts. It will be your personal writing book, for your eyes only.

❏ Refer often to the exercises you completed for this step. They will remind you why it is important to continue.

❏ Picture your readers.

❏ Value your purpose. Remember that you deserve to have your voice heard as much as anyone else.

BEFORE YOU GO ON TO THE NEXT STEP

Give yourself permission to explore your past and reexamine its meaning. Acknowledge that you have the right to tell the story of your life. Don't let your concerns paralyze you.

    Look back often at the reasons you noted for writing your memoir. It will help you value your life experiences. Remind yourself with every chapter who your readers will be. Review in your mind what you hope they will learn and understand from your memoir. You are the only one who can tell your story, and if you don't do it, no one will.

When you are clear about *why* you want to write your memoir, continue to Step 2, where you will decide *what* to write.

CREATIVE CLUSTER

STEP 2

WHAT TO WRITE

"WHAT MATTERS IN LIFE IS NOT WHAT HAPPENS TO YOU,
BUT WHAT YOU REMEMBER AND HOW YOU REMEMBER IT."
—Gabriel García Márquez

PERHAPS YOU ALREADY HAVE SOME IDEAS about the main topic of your memoir. It may be a slice of your life, such as the two years you lived in Paris. It may recount a love affair or the death of a loved one. Or it may cover a longer period of your life that includes your first job as a secretary and follows you as you moved up the ladder to become a partner in the firm.

If you haven't decided on the scope of your memoir yet, that's fine too. It's not necessary to know all that you will cover in your book before you start writing. You will decide what to include during the process of reexamining your life. For now, it's enough to create a list of significant life experiences that will show you where to begin.

When you think about the myriad events in your life, you may rediscover many experiences that look like delectable dishes on a multipage menu. Which ones do you want to taste again? Which are the main courses and which are the side dishes that may be too filling or make you uncomfortable? The exercises in this step will help you make those decisions about how much of your life you want to explore in this memoir.

WHAT IS MEMOIR?

When famous people write about their lives, they often call them memoirs (with an "s" at the end). Memoirs usually span a lifetime. They start at birth and continue through the significant events in adulthood that guided the author to become successful. An "autobiography" is another name for a book written by an author that includes experiences from an entire life.

A memoir (without an "s" at the end) usually covers a segment or period of a person's life, rather than the whole life. Stories center on a unifying theme, such as the span of a marriage, the length of a career, recovery from an illness, or a time of raising children. Most people write this type of memoir. It involves a more manageable task then trying to chronicle an entire lifetime. And the process of focusing on one significant slice of your life can bring great satisfaction.

Some people confuse a memoir with a journal. A journal involves chronicling your thoughts and feelings about what is going on in your life. Journal writing can be a valuable tool for understanding experiences and for letting off steam. Yet a journal makes no attempt to examine life events by creating scenes, stories, and dialogue, which form the basis of modern memoir.

Students in my classes and writing groups have written about a variety of topics:

౼౦ౖ౬౨

Mike wrote about his life in Nigeria in the Peace Corps.

౼౦ౖ౬౨

Lisa wrote about her long recovery from breast cancer.

౼౦ౖ౬౨

Sue wrote about raising her sons after losing her husband in Vietnam.

౼౦ౖ౬౨

Charlene wrote about thirty years of working for an airline.

౼౦ౖ౬౨

Gene wrote about creating a product and starting a company.

౼౦ౖ౬౨

Kathy wrote about taking care of her mother after she had a stroke.

✂◦◯◦✂

Marguerite wrote about raising her profoundly deaf child.

✂◦◯◦✂

Irene wrote about riding the Kindertrain from Austria to England at the start of World War II.

WHAT TO WRITE ABOUT

Exercises on the following pages will help you delve deeper into your own life story to identify the events and experiences you want to include in your book. Try to complete one of these exercises each day during the next week or two. When you finish, go back and review them all.

As you mull over your list of topics, you may find that you want to add more memories to your original ideas. Take your time as you edit your lists to make sure you are enthusiastic about exploring the topics you have chosen. The topics you choose now will become your "go-to" list of ideas when you start to write your memoir.

MAKE A LIST

Lists provide us with quick and easy ways to collect ideas. By using single words or short phrases, we are able to capture memories like lightning bugs in a jar at dusk.

Below are some topic suggestions to help you create lists of the significant events in your life. Start with the first one, and write "Firsts" at the top of a page in your spiral notebook. Then cast your mind back in time.

As the memories pop up, collect them in a list. Then move on to the other topics below and spend as much time as you wish making more lists of ideas for your memoir. See which topics encourage you to remember the most significant life events.

TOPIC IDEAS FOR YOUR MEMOIR

❑ List the firsts in your life—the first time you went to Venice, your first job, the first time you said "hello" to someone, your first kiss, the first time you understood . . . .

❑ Name the most important people in your life that you want to include in your book. Jot down notes for a story about each person.

❑ What were the turning points in your life? List them in order.

❑ Identify the places where important events occurred in your life; describe briefly what happened there.

❑ Inventory your favorite possessions. Write down who gave them to you or where you acquired them.

❑ List your successes. Who or what helped you succeed?

❑ List your disappointments or failures. What did you learn from those experiences?

❑ Make a list of the special places you have visited in your travels. Then go back and jot down what was most interesting to you about each place.

❑ What are your family's favorite stories about you? What are you known for doing or saying?

❑ Make a list of "Goodbyes"—the last times you said goodbye to significant people, places, and experiences in your life.

❑ What stories have you told over and over about your life? What are the stories that other people find most interesting about you?

EXERCISE

MAKE A TIMELINE

A useful way to remember the significant events in your life is to think of them chronologically. This exercise will help you recall events by placing them on a timeline.

On the left side of a piece of paper, list each decade you have been alive in a column, such as 1950s, 1960s, etc. Leave room between each of the decades so you can record the events you remember from that time period. Include the years when the events happened if you can recall them.

Star each event that has a good story associated with it and make a short note to remind yourself of the story.

When you are finished, rewrite your timeline on a clean sheet of paper. Tape it to a wall or put it someplace where you can refer to it often. Following is a brief example of a timeline. Make yours as detailed as you wish.

MY TIMELINE (AN EXAMPLE)

1950s

May, 14, 1953 Born in Wichita, Kansas to May and Charles Cummings—premature/incubator for two weeks at Memorial Hospital.

Dec. 8, 1956

Sister Julia born—I stayed with Grandma Jane; Dressed her cat Milly like a baby.

Sept. 1958

Kindergarten at Jefferson Elem., Wichita, I cried every day for first month.

May 1, 1959

Brother Bobby born. I tried to sell him to a neighbor for five dollars.

1960s

School Days—best friend Joyce, climbed trees, played softball in the street, broke neighbor's window, blamed Bobby, water skied at the lake.

June 1964

Tornado took off our roof while we were in basement; Bobby missing.

I found him under the sink.

1970s

June, 1971

Graduated from Hayward High with honors. In

Glee Club (Sang at Radio City Music Hall in NYC) and Year Book editor—left out faculty pages and got in trouble. Dated John, tennis finals, theater, prom.

July, 1971

Bobby got leukemia. I nursed him all summer.

Sept. 1971

Started at Ohio State U.

Frosh year: choir, weekends with Bobby;

Soph. year: Met Vic, hiked with Bobby at Yosemite, changed major to nursing;

Jr. year: Pres. Nurses Soc., choir

Sr. year: classes and practice at campus hospital; choir concert tour, engaged to Vic.

March 14, 1975

Bobby died

June, 1975

Graduated RN; started work at Memorial Hospital in cancer ward

Nov, 6, 1975

Married Vic

1980s (Etc.)

1990s

2000s

EXERCISE

MAKE A CREATIVE CLUSTER

Some people find they can recall life experiences better if they create a cluster of ideas, rather than listing them in a linear fashion. A cluster diagram gives you the opportunity to spawn a variety of ideas that will add depth to each topic.

To make a Creative Cluster, draw a circle the size of a golf ball in the middle of a clean sheet of paper. Inside the circle, write a short phrase that identifies one of your significant events. For example: "My first job" or "Moving to NYC." This will be the theme of your cluster. (See Creative Cluster example, page 22.)

Then let your mind wander back to that time. Think about what happened and the key peopled involved. Draw radiating lines out from the central circle like spokes. Connect the ends of those spokes with more circles. Write details in the new circles as you remember more images that relate to your central theme.

Think of stories you can tell about each event you write in a circle. Then create more adjoining circles for those circles, writing notes in each about the details of those stories—what happened, who was there, what was said, how you felt, what you wore, what it looked and smelled like.

Spend as much time as it takes with this exercise. When you are finished, choose one circle and write a one-page story from the ideas you have written there. In your story, recreate your experiences with as many details from your circles as possible.

Don't worry about grammar or spelling for now. Just write about your experiences as you remember them. What time of year was it? Where was the sun? Were you inside or outside? What were you wearing? What did the others look like? What did he/she say? How did you feel?

Write it all down. Let it flow. Visualize and recreate that moment.

WRITING PRACTICE

Turn to a fresh page in your spiral-bound notebook and write for ten minutes about one of the topics you identified in these exercises. Try to capture as many details as you can remember.

Pour out your ideas onto the page, like maple syrup onto pancakes. Let it be messy, with run-on sentences if you wish. Keep writing until you have said all you want to say for now about that experience. If you wish, write for ten more minutes about another topic from the worksheet or from one of your exercises.

The stories you write now, no matter how short, will provide building blocks for your memories. You may rewrite them in more detail later. Don't worry about the order when they occurred in your life. Just choose a few stories to write about that interest you now.

SUMMARY EXERCISE

WHAT WILL I WRITE ABOUT?

Now that you have reflected on your life and completed several exercises to help discover what to write about in your memoir, it's time make some decisions. What stories would you really like to tell? How you overcame a bad marriage and moved on? How you raised the boys? How you worked your way around the world as a teacher? What are the most compelling and relevant stories you want to write?

Go back over all of your exercises and ask yourself which experiences you definitely want to include. Make a list of these important topics below or in your spiral-bound writing notebook. Try to come up with ten topics. Keep this list handy; you will refer to it often for new ideas as you begin to write your stories.

THE TOP 10 TOPICS FOR MY MEMOIR

1._____

2._____

3._____

4._____

5._____

6._____

7._____

8._____

9._____

10._____

TIPS

❑ Complete the exercises in this chapter over a series of days rather than all at once.

❑ Look over your lists and memories from the exercises in this step. Use a highlighter to mark the most important events you would like to write about in your memoir.

❑ Make a master list of the most significant life events that you identified. You may be able to use this list as an outline for your memoir.

❑ Create a Top 10 Topics list from all your exercises. These will be the first topics you write about.

❑ Look back at these exercises from time to time as you are writing your memoir. They will help you when you get stuck.

BEFORE YOU GO ON TO THE NEXT STEP:

Once you complete the exercises in this chapter you are well on your way to your goal of writing a memoir. Now you have a list of Top 10 Topics that you want to write about in your book. Keep the list in a special place where you can mine it for ideas.

In the next chapter you will determine the scope of your memoir and create a more detailed plan with a notebook to guide you while you write.

Memoir Notebook

STEP 3

PLAN YOUR BOOK

"TWENTY YEARS FROM NOW YOU WILL BE
MORE DISAPPOINTED BY THE THINGS YOU DIDN'T DO
THAN BY THE ONES YOU DID DO."
—Mark Twain

Now that you have created a preliminary list of the topics you want to include in your memoir, the next step is to organize those ideas into a framework for your book. Each of your topics will represent a story, or perhaps a chapter, in your book. So for now, think of this list of topics as a preliminary table of contents for your memoir. When you start writing, you can use these topics as prompts to give yourself writing assignments.

I'm going to be very directive for the next several pages. Humor me. I have found that most people appreciate having their efforts result in a physical manifestation and watching it grow over time. This is what works for me, but of course you can try any variation that works best for you. The idea is to begin creating something tangible that allows you to see your progress.

A clear-cut way to structure the contents of your memoir is to create an actual book (a three-ring binder notebook) that will contain all of your completed memoir stories in one place. Let's call it your "Memoir Notebook." You will use this notebook to layout the components of your memoir. It will:

❑ become the place where you file your stories after you write them.

❑ be the repository for photos and memorabilia you select to illustrate your memoir.

❑ house all the ideas you jot down in the middle of the night and the relevant articles you have clipped from magazines.

❑ shape the way you make decisions about which scenes to eliminate and which ones to keep.

YOUR "MEMOIR NOTEBOOK"

Your first task in this step is to pay a visit to your local office-supply store and buy a 9" x 12" three-ring binder notebook that has a clear plastic sheet over the cover with room to add a title page. These notebooks come in a variety of colors. Select one that is appealing to you, because this notebook is going to be your close companion as you work on your memoir writing project.

Back at home, write or type a working title for your memoir in big letters on a sheet of 8½" x 11" paper. Your title may be vague right now, such as: JUDY'S MEMOIR. Or it may be more descriptive: LIVING IN GERMANY 1984–87. Don't spend much time thinking about a catchy title right now. The theme of your memoir may shift once you start writing your stories and probing their meaning. A more creative title will come to you later, after you have begun to write. Your Memoir Notebook will be a work in progress. You easily can change the title page as many times as you wish.

Below your working title on the page, write your name after the word "By" to establish yourself as the author. You may want to use colored pencils to decorate your cover page or attach a photo to the sheet. Tuck this title page into the clear plastic sleeve on the cover of your book.

On the spine of your notebook there should be a narrow pocket with a clear plastic cover. Cut out a thin strip of paper and write your working title on it in big enough letters so you can read it from a distance. Place this title strip into the pocket on the spine. That title on the spine will allow you to find your Memoir Notebook easily among the other books standing on your shelf. Its physical presence will remind you of your memoir-writing project and your plan to fill that book with your life stories.

When you have finished creating a cover for your book and claiming ownership of its future contents, pat yourself on the back. Now you have an actual book with a title and your name on it. This is an important first step toward completing your memoir. As the notebook fills with your stories, chapter after chapter, you will view it with satisfaction and confidence. And even if your memoir never is printed as a bound volume or published with an ISBN and barcode, you will have produced an actual book that contains your writing. This is a huge advancement over leaving behind scattered scraps of paper with jotted notes. Your heirs or friends who find this book on your shelf after you are gone will know exactly what it is and what you intended.

Plan the Structure of Your Book

While you are purchasing your notebook at the office-supply store, also buy a package of three-hole-punched divider pages with tabs. You will use these divider pages to separate the stories and chapters that you write for your book. Be sure to select divider pages with plastic tabs for use with inserted titles rather than tabs you write on directly. Tab inserts will give you the flexibility to change chapter titles as your book takes shape.

Now it's time to decide what story titles you will insert into the tabs of those divider sheets. You spent some time in Step 2 determining what stories you want to write about for your memoir. Your list of Top 10 Topics will form your preliminary table of contents and will suggest the titles for your tabs. If you didn't create a list of ten topics for your memoir, do it now. Look back over the exercises in Step 2—the lists, the timeline, the Creative Cluster, and the worksheet. Use a highlighter to identify the stories you most want to tell.

Next, list these ten topics on an 8½" x 11" sheet of paper. Place them in an order that makes sense to you, whether it is chronologically or by theme or in order of their significance. Punch the paper with three holes and put it in the front of your notebook. Now you have a table of contents and a beginning format for your book. As you begin to write your stories and see more clearly the direction of your memoir, you can easily add to or subtract from this list of contents. For now, though, you have a starting point.

If the stories on your list have long descriptive titles, write a brief two- or three-word working title beside each one. Then write these short, abbreviated titles onto the small tabs provided in the package and insert them into your divider pages.

By adding titles to your divider sheets, you have created a reminder to yourself of the stories you want to write. Now, for the first time, you can see how your book will be organized and what topics you will cover.

In the next steps of this book you will build on this structure to compose stories about each of these topics. As you begin writing, you may want to start with the story topic you placed on your first divider sheet or you can skip around and write about a topic you've placed further back in your notebook that interests you most at this time. Make it your goal to complete a story for each of these topics on a schedule, perhaps one each week, or one each month. Then, little by little, you will fill up your notebook and complete your memoir in a timely fashion.

ELECTRONIC FILES VS. HARD-COPY CHAPTERS

If you, like most of us, write your stories using a word processing program, you will need to organize your writing electronically as well. It's a good idea to create an electronic folder in Word (for a PC or an Apple) or in Pages (for Apple), named something like "My Memoir," where you can save all the documents as files. Give each file document a working title so you can find it easily.

You may wonder how these electronic files fit with the hard-copy Memoir Notebook I am suggesting you create. The answer is simple. By printing out your stories and placing them into a notebook, you can see the size and scope of your memoir. Stories saved only on a disk or on computer hard drive may be forgotten or ignored, unlike a real book filled with chapters that sits on your shelf.

Printed chapters will allow you to keep track of how far you've come on your project, as they stack up in your Memoir Notebook. A review of these printed pages will let you see if you have repeated ideas in different chapters or left out important sections. And when you have finished writing your book, you will have a hard copy of the whole memoir that you can edit in its entirety.

So for now, print out each story when you complete it. Punch the pages with three holes and file them in your three-ring Memoir Notebook.

Organize Your Photographs

The final purchase you need to make at that office-supply store is a package of 8½" x 11" clear, acid-free plastic sleeves that are three-hole punched. These sleeves will hold the photographs you want to include in your book.

Some memoir writers structure their books entirely around their photographs, writing stories only about the photos they have selected. Others writers collect a group of photos from the time period of their memoir and include them on a few pages in a chapter or in the middle or end of their book.

However you choose to use them, there is no question that photographs will enhance your book. Start now to collect photographs that relate to the events you plan to write about in your memoir. This project could take some time if you are like most of us, with hundreds of prints and slides stored away in boxes. Perhaps you have placed some of them in scrapbooks already. And if you are really organized, you may have digitized all of your photographs.

Whatever your method of curating your photos, now is the time to sort through them and select the ones that will best illustrate your memoir. You will use these photos in Step 4 to help unlock your memories and in Step 5 to prompt you as you write about your life.

Be sure to choose good quality photos that will reproduce well on a printed page. Select only the best of the best. If your photos are digitized, make a print of each one you want to use on inexpensive printer paper and place it into a plastic sleeve in your Memoir Notebook. Note on the back of the photo where you found it and write down the electronic file number, so you can find it again.

Organize the pictures by topic as you place them in the plastic sleeves. Then file those sleeves behind the dividers for the topics you think the photos will illustrate. If you aren't sure about this yet, put all the photos you plan to use in sleeves at the end of the notebook for now, where you can find them when you are ready to make more decisions about the layout of your book.

EXERCISE

WRITE CAPTIONS

Write captions for each of the photos you plan to use, identifying all the people you can. You may write on the back of the photos, but be sure to write softly with a pencil. A better way to create a caption is to write or type it on a separate strip of paper that is the same width as the photo. Then attach the paper caption to the back of the photo with a small strip of acid-free tape.

This exercise is time-consuming, but it is very important. When you finish, you will be pleased to have all your photos organized in plastic sleeves in your Memoir Notebook where you can find them. The people and events pictured in the photographs will be identified in a caption you have written. Now it will be easy to use these photos to prompt your memories and enhance your descriptions of a scene.

COLLECT MEANINGFUL MEMORABILIA

The addition of memorabilia—certificates, letters, and art work—will enliven your memoir even more. These items add authenticity to your writing and will allow the reader to actually see the evidence behind your stories.

Each of us has kept some important documents, such as a marriage license, birth certificate, passport with country stamps, diploma, or other honor. Consider adding them to your memoir where they will complement your stories. Also look for art work, poems, published articles, and other items created by you or the people in your stories.

Take photos of larger materials, such as your mother's pewter teapot or grandpa's Meerschaum pipe. If you don't have the object anymore, you may be able to find a photo of a similar object in the public domain on the Internet that you can download for use in your book. Scratch around in your files or boxes of "stuff" to see what you can find to add depth to your memoir.

MEMORABILIA IDEAS FOR YOUR BOOK

Letters
Postcards, emails, telegrams, faxes, signed special
    occasion cards
Honors, diplomas, certificates, report cards
Trip itineraries and brochures
Paper money from other countries
Invitations and dance programs

Playbills or concert programs

Sheet music

Poems or other writing

Autographs

Clippings from newspapers or magazines about you
or your family

Birth announcements or certificates

Wedding announcements or certificates

Obituaries, death certificates

Genealogy research and a family tree

Timelines of events in the life of family members

Menus from restaurants for special occasions

Important or historic bills or receipts

Programs from special sporting events

Maps of places mentioned in your book

Favorite or family recipes

Photos of objects such as jewelry or family heirlooms

Personal or meaningful art work

EXERCISE
LIST YOUR MEMORABILIA

Make a list of the memorabilia you want to include in each of your chapters. Take photos of these items and place the photos or a copy of the photos in a plastic sleeve in the appropriate chapter of your Memoir Notebook. Then write a short description of each item that includes what you want to say about it in your story.

WRITING PRACTICE

Select one piece of memorabilia that intrigues you and write a page about it. Describe what you see. What is its meaning to you? How would you explain it to someone else? Is there a story behind it?

When you are finished, three-hole punch the page and put it in your new Memoir Notebook behind the appropriate divider page. You may decide to use this story in the final draft of your memoir or you may rewrite it in a different way.

If you wish, complete this same exercise using other items you plan to include in your book.

TIPS

❏ Buy a 3-ring notebook and make a title page.

❏ Create a preliminary table of contents for this Memoir Notebook out of your list of Top 10 Stories you want to write.

❏ Label notebook dividers with titles for these stories.

❏ Gather photos and pictures of memorabilia in plastic sleeves.

❏ Write a caption for each photo and a brief description of each piece of memorabilia.

Now you have a real, physical book where you can collect the written stories, photos, and memorabilia for your memoir. This three-ring Memoir Notebook contains a table of contents and chapter dividers labeled with working titles of some of the stories you want to tell.

Place your book on a shelf or table where you can see it every day. It will provide you with a visual reminder of your commitment to write your memoir. Now it's up to you to make the time to complete it.

BEFORE YOU GO ON TO THE NEXT STEP

Look back over the topics you have chosen to write about in your memoir. Do you have the divider sheets clearly labeled and the photos you will use for each chapter filed behind them? Let the physical process of creating a Memoir Notebook work in tandem with the mental process of organizing the contents of your memoir. Together these efforts will wipe away the haze of uncertainty that often surrounds the start of a writing project. Once you complete this step, you will see the way forward to complete your memoir.

The next few steps in this book will give you guidance for tapping your memories and writing your stories. As you begin to write, give yourself regular assignments from your preliminary table of contents and start to fill up the pages behind each divider sheet. Use your Memoir Notebook to guide your project to completion.

My Neighborhood

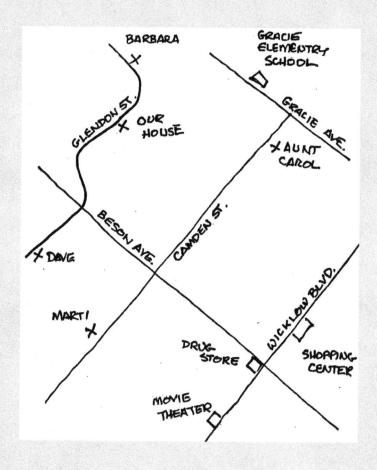

STEP 4

TAP YOUR MEMORIES

"MEMORY IS THE MOTHER OF ALL WISDOM."
— Aeschylus

WHEN YOU READ A WELL-CRAFTED MEMOIR such as Jill Ker Conway's *The Road from Coorain*, Frank McCourt's *Angela's Ashes*, or Annie Dillard's *An American Childhood*, you may think the authors easily remembered all those details of the past with total recall. The writing is so vivid it appears they put pen on paper and the memories just flooded back. The books must have almost written themselves.

Probably not. Memories come to most of us in bits and pieces. They flit through our minds like butterflies on a warm spring day. It's a challenge to catch those memories and pin them down on the page to be preserved.

In this step you will work on capturing your memories of places, people, things, and times. Exercises will suggest a variety of ways to reconstruct the important events of your past. To recall the "place" where events occurred, you can draw a map or even revisit the scene of an event from long ago. To remember the characteristics of the "people" in your stories, you may be able to reconnect with living family members and friends or look at photos of them. To reconnect with the fine points of the "things" in your experience, you can reexamine cherished objects you still own or find similar things at a thrift shop.

Remembering the "times" when events occurred is perhaps most difficult. Sometimes we remember events that took place over a long period of time as only a single experience. Or conversely, we may recall a single experience as a more complex one that took place over many months. We may need the assistance of newspapers, books, and movies to recreate the structure of a time period where we can hang our experiences.

Like an archaeologist, you need to unearth each memory bit by bit from the events of your life. It takes work to find these fragments, dust them off, and look at them in the light of a new day. You need to reconstruct whole events from the pieces you recall. Then you must examine your recollections closely, as with a microscope, in order to see their significance and determine where they fit into the narrative of your life.

One of the best ways to reconnect with memories is to use your senses. From birth, you learn most of your information about the world around you by using the senses of sight, hearing, smell, taste, and touch. If you can access those sensory experiences from your memory, you may have a good chance of recreating entire scenes from your past.

How did Mom's meatloaf taste? What did your spouse look like the day you met? How did the woods near your house smell in spring? What was the timbre of your grandfather's voice? How did your baby's skin feel when you gave him a bath? When you add these sensory images to stories, you will remember a scene more completely, and at the same time you will invite readers to experience your life not from a distance, but close up, just as you did. Remembered elements like these will add surprising spice to plain vanilla stories.

"Memoir" is the French word for memory. In English the word has come to mean a book or a story about a person's past, and it relies completely on the richness of an author's memory to make that past come alive. Successful memoirists dig deep to find the details necessary to create a credible story about the events that shaped them.

Your readers will be able to visualize the house where you spent your childhood if you walk them through it, pointing out the hole in the screen door where the cat came in and showing them the deep gash you made in the dining room wall when you tipped your chair back too far and fell into it. They will see your grandfather clearly if you describe him sitting in a tired armchair wreathed in fragrant pipe smoke, stroking the arm rests with the tips of his fingers until the nubby green fabric is worn smooth.

This step contains a variety of suggestions to help you re-connect with your past. Start with the worksheet to warm up your memory muscles. Then move on to the memory exercis-es that are grouped into four categories to help you recall the places, people, things, and times from your life experience.

WORKSHEET

WHAT DO YOU REMEMBER?

Use this worksheet to begin tapping your memories. Start by choosing one story you want to write. It should be listed in your preliminary table of contents and written on one of the divider tabs in your memoir notebook. Write a working title at the top of the worksheet. Then fill in the blanks. You may want to add more details of your own. Make a copy of this worksheet for each of your stories.

Title or subject of your story: _____

_____

Describe the locations where your story took place:_____

_____

What objects, furniture, and natural elements do you see?___

_____

What are the colors? _____

_____

Do you smell anything? _____

_____

What time of year is it? How do you know? _____

_____

What time of day is it? _____

_____

Does it feel safe? scary? cozy? stark? What elements give you this impression? _____

_____

What sounds do you hear? _____

_____

Who is there?_____

_____

Describe the people—including yourself —(demeanor, cloth-ing, voice, mood). _____

_____

What are you doing? _____

_____

What are you thinking?_____

_____

When does this take place?_____

_____

What else is going on in the world? _____

_____

EXERCISES FOR REMEMBERING PLACES, PEOPLE, THINGS, AND TIMES

Choose one of the stories from your list of Top 10 Topics at the end of Step 2. Take out your spiral-bound writing notebook and write a title for your story at the top of a fresh page.

Now select one of the memory exercises from the following pages. It will provide you with sensory keys to unlock your recollections.

For example, to set the scene of your story, try one of the exercises for remembering places, such as drawing a picture or creating a map of the setting. If you are writing about meeting your spouse in the 1960s, play some music you both enjoyed at that time, perhaps the Beatles or songs from a Broadway show.

As you work on each exercise, take notes to capture the memories that surface. Don't try to write a complete story right now. Just pay attention. What do you see? What do you hear? What are you feeling now? What did you feel then? Write it all down. Use the music, photos, drawings or collages to bring back the images that will make your story come alive again.

For each of the stories you write in your book, use at least one of the suggestions you find on the next few pages to help you recall events before you write about them.

EXERCISE

REMEMBER THE PLACES

❏ Draw a picture of the place where your story occurred. Add all the details you can. Features will come to you as you begin to draw. You may want to draw yourself and other people in the scene. You don't need to know how to draw. You can use simple sketches, but the important thing is to go back to that place and see it in your mind's eye. Use colored pencils or paints if you wish.

Then write a brief description of the images you drew and the stories that you recalled as you were drawing. You may jot down notes for now, capturing the details in a few words. However, if a full-blown story tiptoes into your mind, write it down.

❏ Draw a map of your home, your neighborhood, a childhood bedroom or a workplace. Lay out all the elements you remember about that location. Label important items or locations. Make notes as they occur to you about events that occurred there.

❏ Look at old photographs of the place you are writing about. Examine the photos carefully, looking for details you can use later to describe the background for your events. You may want to include some of these photos in your book.

❑ Cut pictures out of magazines that remind you of a scene you want to remember. See if you can find illustrations that resemble places where you lived or visited. Then make a collage of these images on another piece of paper.

This exercise works especially well for a travel memoir, to help you remember cities and sites you visited. Take notes or label the images. Refer back to this collage when you begin to write your stories.

❑ Go back to the neighborhood, city, or countryside that is the setting of your story. Revisit this place before you start to write about it. Breathe deeply and look around slowly. Close your eyes and listen. Take notes in your spiral-bound writing notebook that will stimulate your memory and provide accurate details for your story. Take photos or sketch the area.

❑ Use Google Earth, Zillow or another online real-estate database to find a photo of a house where you lived or other building, by typing in the address. Explore your old haunts online. Print out the picture. Take notes.

EXERCISE
REMEMBER THE PEOPLE

❑ Examine photographs of the people you will write about. Questions to ask: Who are the people in the picture? What is your relationship to them? Where was the photo taken? What was the occasion for taking the photo? Can you read their body language? Facial expressions? Gestures? Appropriateness of their clothing? What were their motivations at that time? What do you see now that you didn't recognize then?

❑ Examine a photograph of yourself. Select a photo of yourself from the time period you will be writing about in your memoir. Write notes about what you see in that photo. Questions to get you started: Can you read your body language? Facial expression? What were you thinking or feeling when the photo was taken? Is there a backstory to your clothing or to the setting? What did you like or not like about that photo when you first saw it? How do you feel about the picture now?

❑ Draw a sketch of yourself and others in your story. Place yourselves in the scene. Add details. What do you notice about the way you drew these people?

❏ Reconnect with old friends and family. Use the Internet, a phone call, or a letter to interview people from your past. Prepare some questions that will help you write an insightful story. What do they remember about you, other family members, or events? What can you learn about their participation in your life?

❏ Plan a family reunion and interview family members in person who have known you or your parents for a long time. Capture the interview on a video or audio recording. If your relatives are elderly, don't delay. Take notes to describe the people: attitude toward life, tone of voice, clothing, hair and more.

❏ Find old letters and put them into acid-free plastic sleeves to preserve them. You can keep the sleeves together in a three-ring notebook. Read the letters and write a few paragraphs about whatever comes to mind. If they are letters written by you, write about how you felt then or how you feel now about what you said. If they were written by someone else, how did you respond? How would you respond now?

❏ Buy your mother's old perfume and or your dad's old aftershave and wear it for a day while you take notes.

❏ Listen to music you enjoyed with friends or family. Did you hear it at a concert or at a dance with someone? Does it move you now? Take notes.

REMEMBER THE THINGS

❑ Go through those boxes of items you have kept for a long time—Christmas ornaments, theater programs, invitations, etc. Take a photo of them, and write a short description. What stories come to mind? Plan to use the photos in your memoir. Then you can decide: perhaps it is time to give or throw the items away.

❑ Make an inventory of the special objects you have collected over the years, such as a collection of African carvings, Hummel figurines, or Hopi Kachina dolls. Go through your house and take photos of them all. What are the stories behind your collections?

❑ Create a scrapbook or online photo book of these objects with a short description of their background and importance to you. In this way, your heirs will know their significance and be able to make decisions about what to do with them when you are no longer able.

❑ Cook to remember. Bake your mother's lemon meringue pie from the recipe she gave you when you were married. Recreate that Mexican casserole you made for all those summer backyard parties. Savor the smells and tastes of a special meal from long ago.

Take notes. A variation is to return to an old favorite restaurant and order your favorite dish.

❏ Creative visualization. Find a piece of clothing (a hat, a scarf, a jacket) that you wore during the time about which you are writing. Put it on and stand in front of a mirror. Try to imagine yourself as you looked before while wearing that clothing. Write a paragraph about where you might have been going or what you were doing when dressed like that. Try writing it in the present tense. What is on your mind?

❏ Visit a historical museum or a thrift shop to reacquaint yourself with the look of the era when your memoir takes place. You may have forgotten some of the tools, appliances, furniture, clothing and other items that will add authenticity to your writing. Take notes.

❏ Use all your senses to rediscover the delight you once felt in your things. Hold them, touch them, and smell them. Think about the first time you saw each item. Did someone give it to you? Did you find this treasure at a market in Peru or in a hometown shop? Write down your memories. You may be able to create a whole memoir by writing stories about the items that are important to you, such as your cars or special collections.

EXERCISE
REMEMBER THE TIMES

❏ Look at old magazines and newspapers online or at the library. What were the news items and headlines that took place at the same time as your personal story? What was being sold in the ads? In retrospect, do you see now how national and global events influenced you? Think about placing your experiences into the context of the bigger stories that happened around you. Make copies of articles or ads from periodicals and use them as illustrations in your book.

❏ Read a book that describes events you remember from the era you want to recall. See if you can gain new insights to give a better perspective to your story. What was the mood of the time? What did people talk about and worry about?

❏ Reread a favorite book that you read years ago. Do you remember where you were when you read it before? How did it affect you then versus now?

❏ Listen to music from the era of your life you want to write about and see what dances onto the pages of your notebook.

❑ Use photos to research the era. Find fashion details that will make your writing more authentic. Look carefully at room décor, clothing, cars, and hair styles in your photos. Use those details to describe events and provide accurate imagery.

❑ Use the Internet to research the history of your time period. Search for events that occurred when your story takes place. For example, if you are writing about personal experiences that happened at the time of the 1960s Civil Rights Movement or the 9/11 attacks, find details to add background and a context to your story.

❑ Look at websites that have photos of places, houses, objects, clothing, or cars from your time period. For example, if you are writing about a trip on Highway 66 in the family Buick, find websites with photos of the highway and Buicks from that era. Or if you write about a Tupperware Party, look at the Tupperware website to remind yourself of the colors, shapes, and names of those iconic plastic bowls.

❑ Rent a movie that takes place during the era of your story. Pay attention to the way people are dressed, how they talk, what they talk about, what they laugh at, their cars, and the décor of their homes and offices.

SUMMARY EXERCISE
CAPTURE MEMORIES FOR EACH STORY

As you write each of the stories for your memoir, return to this step for suggestions to tap more memories. You may want to try different exercises for each of your stories. The time you take to recall the details of your life experiences will pay dividends in the richness and authenticity of your writing.

TIPS

❏ Use all your senses to bring back memories before you write.

❏ Choose suggestions from each of the four categories (Places, People, Things, Times) to gather memories before you write each story.

❏ Keep a notepad nearby and by your bed at night, ready to capture the memories.

BEFORE YOU GO ON TO THE NEXT STEP

Are you still with me? The act of consciously trying to remember the details of your life events can be difficult, but also rewarding. I hope you have had some fun tripping down memory lane too.

Now you can move on to step 5 and learn more about how to use those memories to tell your life stories.

FIRST DRAFT

From the time I was old enough to know there was a world beyond Indiana, I wanted to see it. My favorite childhood books included Johanna Spyri's _Heidi_, about a girl who lived among the craggy Swiss Alps instead of cornfields; and Rudyard Kipling's _Kim_, which explored the life of a boy in a magic sultan's world called India. I would dream about traveling to those faraway places where I, too, could encounter exotic experiences.

When I graduated from college with a degree in education, those dreams became a concrete plan. I would work my way around the world as a teacher. I would live and teach for a year or two in a city on each of the major continents and travel to enchanted

STEP 5

START WRITING

"Good memoirs are a careful act of construction...
Memoir writers must manufacture a text,
imposing narrative order on a jumble
of half-remembered events."
—William Zinsser
Inventing the Truth: The Art and Craft of Memoir

ONCE YOU HAVE CHOSEN THE LIFE EVENTS you want to write about and have rediscovered some memories of those events, it's time to start writing your memoir. This is the most exciting step of all, because now you will begin to see your book take shape.

If you've tried your hand at creative writing before, you probably are ready to begin. All you need are a few suggestions coupled with a little push from the nest, and you will take off.

On the other hand, if you haven't written much, you may be hesitant and unsure about launching into this writing project. Perhaps you just don't know where to start. You may have struggled with writing at school. Maybe some insensitive person told you that you weren't a very good writer. Or as an adult, you have written only for business or academia.

This I know: The fact that you want to write about your life means that you will find the ability to do it. If you can tell your stories orally, you can write about them too. Writing isn't that different from speaking. It's just another way of expressing yourself. The more you write, the better you will write. Writing is a craft. The only way to improve your craft is by doing more of it.

This step will give you a few pointers about writing to get you started. Try these suggestions and see which ones work best for you. We all write differently, but our aim with writing memoir is the same: to create a coherent narrative out of a myriad of life experiences. To do that, we must deal with disorderly memories that lie scattered in our brains, like railroad cars after a train wreck. They may sprawl in disarray on the surface or they may be buried in a confused heap. Some are worth saving, others are best left alone. It's up to you, the writer, to select the most crucial and pertinent memories and then line them up in an orderly fashion on a narrative track to tell your life story.

WHERE DO I BEGIN?

The most important advice I can give you is that you must show up and write on a regular basis if you really want to write your memoir. There is no trick to it. Seasoned writers know that to get the job done, you must apply the seat of your pants to the seat of your chair. In other words, the only way to write is sit down and do it. Like learning any skill, you need to practice. Whether it's playing the piano or skiing, you must work at it and make mistakes before you will improve. I wish you could learn to write through osmosis or good intentions, but it just doesn't work that way.

You already are well on your way. You've done the preliminary work of choosing the topics you want to write about and you've dredged up memories for those topics, so now you just need to transfer your thoughts onto the page. Now it's time to sit down and write your stories, starting with A–B–C.

A: ASK YOURSELF TO PICTURE THE SCENE

Find a place where you can sit alone comfortably for about an hour. Open your spiral-bound writing notebook to a new page. With a pen you like, write the title of one of your topics at the top of the page. Now think about the scene you are going to write.

Review the memory exercise(s) you completed for this topic. If you didn't complete one of the exercises yet, do it now to picture the scene. If you drew a picture of the location, focus now on the details. What did the living room look like in that apartment you rented on 28th Street? What kind of furniture did you have? What were the colors? What was the view from the window? If you drew a map of the place where your story takes place, review it now. Retrace that route you walked from home to school. Where did you meet your friend each day? Where was that hole in the fence you crawled through for a shortcut?

Imagine you are watching a movie or a play. The curtains open, the lights come up, and you are on stage. Where are you? Who is with you? What do you see?

B: Begin to Write the First Draft

Now put your pen on the paper and record what you see. Keep your hand moving and don't stop until you have finished telling your story. Don't worry about grammar or spelling or the way it sounds for now. Your goal is to write a first draft of your story. Write the scene as though you were telling a friend about the incident after it happened.

Your first draft will not be perfect. No one writes perfectly the first time. Writing is about getting the first draft down on paper and then rewriting it later to make it better. So for right now, push your inner critic aside and just write your story without stopping until you are done.

When you finish, write the words "First Draft" on the top right side of the first page with the date. Then, punch three holes in your pages and file your story in your Memoir Notebook. Resist the impulse to go back and rewrite it now. Wait until some time has passed—at least a day or two—before you reread the story. Let it simmer for a while as the flavors mellow. Wisdom and hindsight are the gifts of time.

C: Correct and Revise

When you read your story again later, you will be able to see where you might make some revisions. Steps 6, 7, 8, and 9 in this book will help you revise your first draft to create a stronger and more masterful story.

Right now, though, you just need to complete the A–B parts of this writing practice. In other words, picture the scene and write the first draft. This first draft will help you get in touch with what you want to say. It will provide the foundation of your story. Later you will add the walls and the roof to create the completed structure.

Just A–B–C? Don't I Need Some Techniques?

You may be wondering if writing is as easy as that. I didn't say it was easy to write, but the process is simple. You really don't need any "techniques." As I said, you will learn to write better just by writing.

However, since I know you may be hungry for more writing instruction, I'll share two basic writing methods that many writers use. Keep in mind that writing is a very individual skill. There is no one correct way to write. Just as with painting or playing a musical instrument, writers use a variety of processes to create a masterpiece. How you write will be your individual choice.

The two methods I offer in this chapter will help you write your first draft. Experiment with both of them and then decide which one works best for you. You can find many excellent books that offer writing instruction, and I recommend you read some of them if you want to learn more. (See suggested Readings at the end of this book.)

PLANNED WRITING METHOD

For this method, you will create a road map or a list of events to guide you. It doesn't need to be a detailed outline or a rigid list. Think of it as the directions you get when you type your destination address into a website such as Google Maps or MapQuest. The list will tell you where to turn and when to continue in a certain direction. It will work like a flow chart to help you remember the parts of the story you want to include and the order in which you want to tell them. It will keep you from getting lost and help you stay on the right road until you reach the end of your story.

To use this Planned Writing method, choose one story from your list of the Top 10 Topics. Reread the list of detailed images you identified for that topic from your memory exercises in Step 4. Then picture the scene and jot down the main points of your story in the order you want to tell them. This will serve as your road map.

For example, you might visualize your sister on that backyard tree swing, her long brown hair flying out behind her as she sticks her legs out and pumps the swing higher. You can hear her shouts of joy. You hear a crack and watch her fall, her arms and legs a-flutter, before she lands in a heap on the grass, the wind momentarily knocked out of her, one arm lying at an odd angle.

A ROADMAP EXAMPLE

Warm spring day, breeze blowing
I push sister Gina in swing
Gina pumps high on rope tree swing, wooden seat
Long brown hair flying, blue dress, she pumps higher,
*   shouts—high voice*
Crack! Rope breaks, I watch in slow motion
She sails to the ground, fluttering like an injured bird
Lands in heap, arm at odd angle
I run to her, she doesn't move
I yell for Mom, who runs out of house, back door slams
Mom does CPR, neighbor hears my screams and calls
*   an ambulance*
Gina coughs and gasps for breath, arm hurts—broken
Mom and Gina go to hospital. Gina OK. She
*   blames me.*

EXERCISE

PLANNED WRITING

Write one of your stories using the "Planned Writing" method. First, create a road map or flow chart like the one above for one of your stories. Make it as detailed or as loose as you wish. Now start writing. Write a few sentences about the first item on your list. Then write about the second item and continue writing until you have told your whole story, using this list to make sure you include all the details and tell the whole story.

WORKSHEET

Planned Writing

Use this worksheet to capture all the details you want to write into your story. Add other images here from your memory exercises in Step 4. Then write a chronological list of events on another piece of paper to serve as a road map to guide you when you write.

The scene I will write today (describe in a few words): _____

_____

My working title: _____

Who are the people in this scene with me? How did they influence me?

_____

What happened? Write a brief summary. _____

_____

Where did the scene take place? Describe the visual details.

_____

_____

When did it happen? Approximate date or time of year:

_____

What was its impact on me? What did I think about it? How did I react? _____

_____

_____

Spontaneous Writing Method

For this method you will write without any notes to guide you. Instead, you will picture the scene, put your pen on the paper, and start writing. If you don't know what to write at first, start by writing some questions on the page: "What did the scene look like? What do I want to say about this topic? What really happened? What was I thinking about then?"

Be patient. Keep your pen on the page. Write whatever comes into your mind. Little by little your hand will pick up speed as you finally launch into the heart of your experience. With no outline other than a general memory of a scene, you may be surprised by what you write and what you learn from it. You may write about something you had forgotten about completely. Some writers find they remember more and dig deeper into the meaning of an event if they don't make plans before they write.

To stay with the car metaphor while considering this spontaneous writing method, picture yourself on the road again. This time, you don't know exactly where you are going. You are out for a joy ride, or you could say you are on a "Joy Write." You have a general idea of the story you want to tell, but you don't know where you will end it or how you will find your way to your destination. You are open to discovery as you explore the back roads of your past. You may veer off into a forgotten memory as you take turns that appeal to you. Continue to follow your instincts and see where they take you.

To get started with this writing technique, choose one of the Top 10 Topics from Step 2. Start with the story that interests you most. Reread your jotted notes about that story from the memory exercises in Step 4. Sit down with your spiral notebook or at the computer keyboard and write the working title of your story at the top of the page. Spend a few minutes picturing the scene.

Now it's time to write what you see. Start wherever you want and write as long as you want. You may want to set a timer and write for at least fifteen minutes. Once you start, keep going. Don't pick up your pen or take your fingers off the keyboard until you are finished. Don't worry about grammar or spelling. Write the action and the details as they come to you. You're cruising down a wide highway with no traffic. Just tell your story.

This kind of writing may be unsettling at first, because you don't know where it will take you. Give it a chance, though, and be on the lookout for the images and stories that pop up unbidden from around the bend. They may reveal a long-forgotten theme that begs to be explored.

Exercise
Spontaneous Writing

Write one of your stories using the spontaneous writing method. Before you start to write, picture the scene you want to capture. What is the setting and who are the people there with you? Then start writing and see what comes out. Don't stop to censor yourself. Keep writing until you have told the whole story. You may not end up writing about the story you started to tell. You may write a piece that is more prescient than your original idea. Maybe it needed to be said. Don't second guess it. Rejoice that you put something on paper. Punch your papers with three holes and put them in your memoir notebook. You will have time to revise later.

WHAT IF I DON'T LIKE WHAT I WRITE?

Whether you use a planned or spontaneous method to create your first draft, remember that your inner critic has no business interrupting your flow. The first time you write about one of your life experiences, it will not pour onto the page or computer screen as a perfect narrative. I don't know any writers who can do that, even those who have been scribbling down their thoughts for years. Most of us start by writing a first draft that lets the thoughts tumble out, without worrying about how they sound or if they tell a good story. For the first draft, we just strive to tell a story just as we would if we were talking to a friend.

What's important for you in this step is to write without stopping until you get a first draft down on paper. This uses your right brain, the seat of creativity. If you stop, your thoughts will immediately switch to the left brain where that darn critic lives. Don't give that bully an inch. Just keep writing, even if you have to use "and" between every sentence to keep going. Your critic may be useful later when you want to revise and edit, but for now, you just need to get the story out. Write about what happened and how you felt about it. Write about your optimism, your fears, your misery, your joy. Don't worry about checking facts and names when you write. You can go back and fill in those details later.

When you finish, read it over and put it away. You will come back to it later with fresh eyes. You may be surprised then at how much better it sounds than you thought it would. If you wish, you can revise it then, or start over and write it again. No one else can tell you how many times you need to write this story. You will learn each time and your writing will improve.

WRITE WITH PEN AND PAPER OR A COMPUTER?

Some writers always write their first drafts by hand, while others insist on typing their drafts on a computer from the start. The first group claims there is a connection between the brain and a hand (with a pen) that facilitates the transfer of thoughts to the page. They think the hand concentrates the mind and the very act of moving your hand across paper enables you to access the mind's deepest thoughts. Other writers, who are used to tapping quickly on a keyboard, feel better able to keep up with the lightning speed of their thoughts by typing.

Whether you write a first draft by hand or by typing, just remember to keep writing without correcting yourself. The first draft needs to flow from your mind without your inner critic telling you to choose another word or to back up and fix a typo. When typing on a computer, where typos can happen quickly, there's a greater temptation to stop and make those corrections as you go. For that reason, many writers prefer to create a first draft with longhand on paper. They train themselves to keep the pen moving as they write, without crossing out or changing words. Later, they revise the first draft and type the second one. Try both methods for your first drafts —writing by hand or typing on a computer keyboard—to see which works best for your own creative writing.

OTHER METHODS FOR TELLING YOUR STORIES

If writing a first draft story still seems too difficult, there are other methods for telling about your life experiences that you can use to create a memoir. Here are a few alternative ideas:

❑ Write your story as a letter to someone in the future

You may find the idea of writing about your life less difficult if you write it in the form of a letter. Letter writing is a familiar activity to most of us. You may want to think of it as writing a long email. Write to someone who you think may want to read about your life in the future, such as a grandchild. Use a piece of stationery for this approach. Be sure to date and sign it. Picture this child reading your story someday. Write as though you were telling your story out loud.

When you finish, you may want to actually mail the letter, or keep it in a plastic sleeve in your Memoir Notebook for now. Later, you can type up all your letter-stories and create a book. Or you can bind the actual letters, written in your own handwriting, into a uniquely personal memoir book.

❏ Write a letter to someone from your past.

Write a letter to a parent, grandparent or some other person who has been an important influence in your life. Even if that person is no longer living, the act of writing a personal letter to him or her may help you put your stories on paper.

❏ Write a letter to yourself.

Write a letter to yourself at the age you were when the events of your story occurred. For example, write a letter about your first job with adult responsibilities to the 21-year-old you. How did you feel about your experiences at that time? How do you feel about them now? Writing a letter to yourself can help you see how much you have matured in the ensuing years. Perhaps it will allow you to view your earlier actions with new compassion and understanding.

❏ Speak your story rather than write it.

Modern technology can save you from writing. One solution is to dictate your stories into a recording device and have someone transcribe your words onto typed pages for your book. Computer programs also will transcribe the words you speak into a microphone and the accuracy of these programs is increasing.

❑ Create a Video.

Have someone make a video of you telling your stories. This can be a priceless gift to your family members, who can watch it for generations to come, although they may need to transfer it to new technology in the future. Before you turn on the camera, jot down notes to yourself about memories you want to include. You also could write a list of questions for an interviewer to use. Some people create a video in addition to their written memoir and tuck a DVD into a plastic sleeve in the book.

START NOW

However you decide to tell your stories, don't delay any longer. Chose a topic today and write a first draft. When you finish, pat yourself on the back. You've taken a first step toward becoming the author of your memoir. You've proven you can do it. Like the first time you took the family car out for a spin by yourself, you may have been unsure, but you did it. You may have hit a few bumps in the road. You may have steered off course. Yet you made a start. As you did then, you will gain in confidence and mastery as you do this again and again.

Make a pact with yourself to sit with pen in hand or with fingers poised over a computer keyboard, for at least an hour at a time—maybe once a day? Twice a week? Find a time that works well for you. Early morning? After dinner? How much do you really want to write your memoir? It takes discipline. That is how every book is written. Authors chip away at it, scene by scene, until an entire book is finished. It's not romantic or magical. It's a process.

Give yourself assignments each week. Little by little, you will write your memoir. Soon it will be more than a bunch of ideas jotted on scraps of paper. You will have the beginnings of an actual book, calling to you to write more pages and actually finish it. Don't fret that it may not be as well written as you imagined it. You will continue to work on it and edit it until it is completed. If you really want to write a story about your life, you WILL be able to do it. Your desire and enthusiasm will carry you through.

Set a goal for when you want to finish your memoir. Maybe you have a wedding anniversary coming up? Or a significant birthday? Perhaps you want to complete it by the holidays to give as a present? With a completion date in mind, you will have fresh incentive.

Get started now. The writing is already inside you. All you have to do is step aside and let it come out.

Tips

❑ Before you write a scene, picture it as though you were watching a scene in a movie.

❑ Start writing now. Don't worry about grammar or the way it sounds. Just write.

❑ When you finish your first draft, put it in your three-ring notebook and don't look at it again for a while. You will edit it later.

❑ Show up to write on a regular schedule. Choose your time and space.

❑ Create a deadline for completion of your memoir. Write your goal in a calendar.

❑ Read other memoirs and note how authors describe their scenes.

BEFORE YOU GO ON TO THE NEXT STEP

Write at least three stories before you go on to the next step. Let your writing flow like a cherry-red convertible breezing along a smooth, wide highway on a sunny day. You are in that car with the top down. No one else is on the road and nothing will stop you. Feel good about yourself. You are actually writing about your life. Don't worry about engine knocks and occasional potholes. You can polish your writing later. Just keep your foot on the gas and go.

One Day . . .

One Day

    One day stands out from the blur of days while I was raising my son and also trying to juggle part-time work and volunteer commitments. I had parked in front of the elementary school at 3:15 on a rainy day, ready to pick up Michael and his friend Jason. I had planned this afternoon down to the minute. First we would head to the barber for Michael's haircut. Then the boys would play at home while I baked 12 dozen cookies for the school bake sale. Later that night I was to host a board meeting at our house.

    All went well until we came out of the barber shop. The rain had stopped. I had parked the car in a dirt lot dotted with puddles. As we reached the car, Jason spied a nearby puddle and jumped into it. The ensuing splash shot toward me like a water cannon, drenching my sweater and leaving clots of mud dangling in my hair.

    Jason mumbled, "Sorry," but I could tell by his eyes that he thought I was an amusing sight. I accepted his apology and mentally added washing his pants to my to-do list.

    At home, I made sure the boys had plenty of Legos to stay busy in the family room when I started baking. Maybe it was because my old mixer made so much noise that I didn't hear the boys giggling and flushing the toilet until I saw the water seeping down the hall into the kitchen from the direction of the bathroom. I shut off the mixer and

STEP 6

BECOME A STORYTELLER

"THE EVENTS IN OUR LIVES HAPPEN IN A SEQUENCE IN TIME,
BUT IN THEIR SIGNIFICANCE TO OURSELVES
THEY FIND THEIR OWN ORDER..."
—Eudora Welty

THE PURPOSE OF THIS STEP is to help you tell a compelling story about your life. It contains suggestions for writing specific stories about your experiences, rather than telling about them in general. Stories give you a frame for writing about your experiences. They focus random events into a structure that provides clear pictures of what took place. Narrative stories recapture your past experiences in 3D by recreating the scenes of your life instead of describing them.

Storytellers have always played an important role in human society, starting with people sitting around a communal campfire. Storytellers are the ones who keep history alive so we can learn from our past and understand the direction of our lives. The stories they tell entertain, educate, and convey moral values. Story telling is vital to the human spirit. It endures today in movies, TV, YouTube videos, and, for the foreseeable future, with the written word.

Today's readers love stories as much as ancient people did. They want stories with drama and tension. They don't want to read vague descriptions about a life; they want enthralling and meaningful stories.

In the previous steps of this book I use the word "story" to refer to the accounts you are writing about your life. Now we are going to take your writing to the next level by focusing on how to write your account as a narrative story. To do this, we will discuss how you can add the elements of storytelling to make your writing more vivid.

When you look back over the stories you have written so far, you may find that they are actually a summary of your experiences. Many first-time memoir writers describe past events in a bare-bones narrative that is short on details and drama. In my first attempt to write memoir, I wrote about my entire adult life in twelve pages of colorless descriptions.

This step will focus on adding narrative structure to your stories so you can tell them in an engaging way. You may just need to slow down and add more details to flesh out a plot. It takes time to set the scene of a story and draw the reader into the action. It takes time to reconnect with the lively images and gripping tension that will reanimate your story for those who weren't there when the events occurred.

Your readers will be disappointed if you write an outlined history of your life. They will know they are not getting the full story if you dismiss your teenage summers by writing, "I always had a good time at the lake when our family rented a cabin there every year in July."

They want to read some good stories about your experiences there. They want to picture you, as a teenage girl, with the neighbor boy who gave you your first kiss—underwater —and then asked you to marry him there fifteen years later. They want to learn about the time you, as a nine-year-old boy, saved your young cousin from drowning after he fell off a slalom waterski and hit his head. They want to relive that starry night when you cooked s'mores over an open campfire with your brothers while your dad told ghost stories that you still can recite to this day.

Before you proceed with learning about the elements of good storytelling, I hope you have written a first draft of at least three stories. Those first drafts may be messy, but they probably contain spontaneity and authenticity. You will want to preserve that energy when you revise your stories.

I didn't want you to think about the elements of storytelling when you wrote those first drafts. The first draft is not the time to ask yourself questions such as: Is this interesting? Why am I writing about that? Have I revealed enough about my feelings when Sue walked out? You don't want to second guess every thought as you write. Most authors find it impossible to write and edit at the same time.

If you have written some first drafts, though, now you can work on adding drama, tension, and structure to your writing. This involves left- and right-brain thinking. It should be attempted only after you have written a first draft.

HOW TO ADD STORIES

You can compare the writing and editing process to being a pastry chef. When you finished your first draft, you made the dough. Then you let it sit for a while. Now it's time to pull it out again and look at it with fresh eyes. It's time to knead the dough, punch some parts down, and allow the best ideas to rise.

To begin, choose one of the stories you wrote that already is sitting snugly in your three-ring Memoir Notebook. Read it over. Is it an interesting story? Do you think others will enjoy reading it? Ask yourself what parts quicken your pulse. Which ones bring you to the brink of tears? Keep those. They probably tell a story. Your readers will identify with those stories too.

Do you show through action how you changed and grew during the events that you describe? If not, don't worry. You have the essence of a good story down on paper. Now all you need to do is add some structure to your story to make it come alive.

See if you find a place in that story where you begin to gallop through your life experiences, telling about events in general and leaving out the details. At that place, start a new paragraph with "One day . . . " or "One time . . . " or "I remember . . . ."

Hover there for a few minutes. Focus in closely. See if you can remember one specific story to tell about what happened there. Transport us back to that time. Let us experience the drama that happened "one time" and see who you were then.

When you say, "One time . . . " or "One day . . . ", we readers take in a quick breath and sit up with anticipation, ready to be immersed and entertained by a story about your life experience, written in the first person, by you.

HOW TO WRITE A COMPELLING STORY

You must take all the scattered memories from your life and create a narrative out of them. Life is disorganized and messy, but you need to mold it into a story that flows in a neat order. This is the memoirist's task, to construct an engaging plot that includes the important points found in scattered memories. In addition, a memoirist must decide which bumps in the road of life were minor and should be ignored. Sometimes a writer may need to change the sequence of events to make the story more captivating, or telescope two experiences that were somewhat similar into one story.

Maybe your husband, Brian, asked you to marry him before you were sure it was right for you, although you did say "yes." You eventually broke off the engagement to be with someone else, but then an event occurred that convinced you Brian was the right one for you. You went back and forth between two men in your life until you made the final decision. Your story may have more punch if you shorten the indecision and leave out some events while retaining the truth of the experience.

As a memoirist, you must always tell the truth and not embellish your stories. They must adhere to your experiences as you remember them. What you need to do is remain faithful to your essential memory of those events and the outcomes they led to, as you structure your story.

Two ways to create stories with structure:

NARRATIVE STORIES NEED A BEGINNING, MIDDLE, AND END

Beginning: Set the scene. Put us there. Start the story just when it gets interesting, just when someone says something that made a difference. Write the important details that will recreate the incident in full color for your reader. Begin with a good lead to grab the reader's attention, such as: "When I was nine, I learned to drive a car." Or "It was the last time I saw my dad, although I didn't know it, of course."

Middle: This is where most of the action takes place. You have enticed the reader in, now you need to tell the story scene by scene. Fill in the details. Here is where you show your arc—how you reacted from the beginning, what you learned, and how you changed. The story must come to a climax that lets us see why the story was told. For example: If your story is about how you ran away from home, did you include a scene that finally showed you the consequences of your actions? Or if your story is about your time as a caregiver for your mother, did you show what you learned from that experience before she died?

End: Readers like to find a satisfying conclusion. Here is where you tie up loose ends and deal with the unanswered questions that remain. Or you can tease your readers by leaving them hanging at the end and anxious to go to the next chapter. "I thought that would be the end of it, but then John walked back into my life in June and nothing would be the same again."

EXERCISE

INSERT A STORY

Choose one of the chapters in your Memoir Notebook that you already wrote as a first draft. Find a place to insert a specific story. Divide your recollections of that story into three sections to create a beginning, middle and end.

Start writing the story with the words "One time..." or "I remember..." Then write the story with an arc that takes you from one place at the beginning through a series of events and ends with a conclusion that shows how you changed and gained new understandings.

Your story may be chronological or not. See how it flows. The important thing is to recreate the events of your life in an engaging narrative that remains true to your experience of those events.

CREATE A "W" PLOT STRUCTURE

Another writing tool often used by fiction writers or script writers is the W or WWW plot design. With this structure, the writer starts the action at the top left of the "W." The main character (in the case of memoir, YOU) exists in a good place, perhaps on top of the world. This sets the scene. Life is going well, with no big problems on the horizon. Then things begin to fall apart and the character (you) slides down that slippery slope of the "W" into a difficult situation at the bottom. The hero or heroine (you) doesn't stay at the bottom for long, though, and soon begins to climb back up the next slope with determination to reach the top again. That can be the end of the story, using a "V" plot structure. Or you may have another setback to write about that brought you back down to the bottom. Then you can describe how you scrambled back up to the top once more.

The interesting action in your story takes place on the slopes—how you rose to success at the top and how you fell from grace to the bottom. This simple plot structure will ensure that you tell an interesting story, using tension and conflict to keep readers reading. You can show both the obvious action and the action that happens beneath the surface. The interplay of these two observations creates the tension that makes the story interesting. You allow readers to wonder about and learn how you overcame the obstacles you describe.

The "W" plot structure will keep readers interested and also allow you to gain new insights into that part of your life, as you put yourself back into the drama again. Break up the tension from time to time. Slow down and don't rush through it. Add some details. Show us the light playing on Richard's curly hair and how you noticed his eyes start to moisten as you talked. Tell us how you felt about what was happening. This will give us the chance to catch a breath before you raise the tension once more and tell Richard that your child isn't his.

Good stories usually have a problem, a conflict or a mystery to be solved. If you use a "W" plot structure to tell your stories, you will keep your readers engaged and pulling for you to win. They want to know how you solved your issues so they can learn and be inspired.

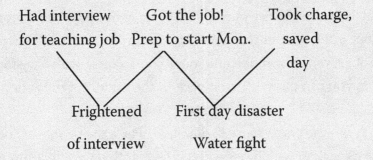

OTHER WAYS TO ADD STRUCTURE AND TENSION

❑ Create a story board. This works well for writers who think visually. Create a small sketch on 3 x 5 cards of each incident that occurs in your story. Then you can move the sketches around until you have arranged them into your desired plot structure. In the process, you may discover more details to include in the story, such as how people dressed and how one scene led to another. A simple way to create a notebook-sized story board is to draw your sketches on Post-it notes that you place onto an open manila folder or an 8½ x 11" piece of paper.

❑ Write your story from the third person point of view, using "he" or "she" instead of "I." In other words, write your story as though you are a narrator telling the events of your life from the outside. This helps if you are having difficulty writing about your own personal relationships with the people in your story. Perhaps you and your brother never got along. It may be easier to get out of your own skin and write a story about your relationship with him from the point of view of an observer. If you become more comfortable with the story later, you can place yourself back in the middle of the action.

❑ Write the entire story in dialogue. Have the people in your story speak to each other with no description or reflections by you. Write as though you are recording their speech in real time, as they (and you) talk to each other. This method essentially will change your story into a screen play and allow you to speak your truth in a loud voice. As you write it, picture yourself sitting in the audience, watching the action unfold.

❑ Start your scene in the middle of the action to grab your reader's attention. You may need to write a lead-up to that important moment, but then you can discard the introductory information when you edit the story later. Be alert for the moment in your story when you are in conflict or when events get exciting. That's where you should start your story.

In summary, try to inject some vivid narrative stories into your writing. Show how you resolved conflicts, fulfilled dreams, and overcame roadblocks to your success. Others will want to read about how you dealt with those problems. You not only will tell your tale, but you'll also share your emotions and pass along your wisdom.

Don Hewitt, the producer of the *60 Minutes* television show, was known for a four-word sentence: "Tell me a story." Hewitt wanted the show to be a different kind of news program, not telling the news, but showing what happened, with a story. He always felt that good stories were the secret to the show's amazing success over the decades. The segments were never boring. They grabbed audience attention with dramatic narratives.

When you become a storyteller, you will do the same thing. The stories already exist inside you. All you need to do is write them down. Your memoir will contain a string of stories about your life. Think of each story as a photographic image and the whole memoir as a slide show or a Power Point presentation of those images.

TIPS

❏ Always write the first draft of your story before you think about revising it.

❏ When you do reread your account, see if you can find a place to insert a narrative, dramatic story.

❏ Structure your stories with a beginning, middle, and end or use a "W" plot.

❏ When you have difficulty remembering a specific narrative story, write the words: "One day . . . " or "I remember . . . ." See what follows.

❏ Look back over your memory exercises for more story ideas.

BEFORE YOU GO ON TO THE NEXT STEP

Write narrative stories about your life experiences for each of the scenes you have written so far. Once you start writing stories that show yourself in action, you will find it easier to do. No longer will you just be recounting events; you will be in the middle of the action. That's what life is all about. Writing about it will stir your blood and endear you to readers in the future. The next step will teach you how to enliven the other people who share the stage with you in your narrative stories.

DIALOGUE

"They've overbooked our flight," Brian said.

"But it's our honeymoon," I said. "What about our hotel reservations for tonight?"

"Don't worry, darling. I'm sure we'll eventually get there and the hotel will give us a refund."

"OK. What happens now?" I didn't want him to see my anxiety.

Brian took my hand. "Let's find a ticket agent and see what they can do for us."

STEP 7

WRITING ABOUT PEOPLE

"THE MAN WHO WRITES ABOUT HIMSELF AND HIS OWN TIME IS THE ONLY MAN WHO WRITES ABOUT ALL PEOPLE AND ALL TIME."
—George Bernard Shaw

THE PEOPLE YOU WRITE ABOUT deserve extra care from you. As the writer of your memoir, you are the chronicler of events they participated in, too. These are people who shaped the person you are today or you wouldn't be writing about them. Others who read your memoir may not know these people. It's up to you to portray them honestly.

Trying to breathe life into a personality on the page is a bit like finding shells on the beach. You pick one up and marvel at its individuality. You wonder what life was like for the creature living in that intricate house. Yet the shell can't tell you.

It takes a thoughtful writer to understand and explain what is inside that shell—to reanimate a person. You, as the writer, must not only describe a person accurately, but also show us the motivations you think were behind their actions. In this step we will consider three ways to make the people in your stories more memorable: Description (use sensory details); Action (reveal motivations); Dialogue (create spoken words that relay intent).

Before reading on, select one of the stories from your Memoir Notebook. Reread it, paying particular attention to the way you portray people. Then read the following three suggestions and see if you can rewrite that section to animate those people and reveal more about them.

Use Sensory Details

One of your goals as a memoir writer is to create an authentic portrayal of the people in your stories by using descriptive images that will generate lively pictures in the reader's mind. The best way to get in touch with descriptive images is to use all your senses. Describe the way a person looks, the sound of the voice, the touch of a hand, and if relevant, a typical smell. Add the catch of recognition in your mother's throat when you tell her what happened. Let us hear a whisper of forgiveness or a guffaw of insinuation. Let us see her pull at the hair behind her ears when she talks to you. Describe the timbre of her voice and the way she smells when she bathes and changes her clothes each afternoon before your father comes home from work. Let us feel the warmth of her hug.

Review the memory exercises for "Remembering the People" from Step 4. In your first draft, did you include any of those details? Think about what images you could add to your descriptions of each person. Look again at photos and letters. Pick up the phone and interview someone who can answer your questions. Select the most telling and revealing details you find to animate the people in your memoir.

WORKSHEET

GATHER DETAILS

Make copies of this worksheet to use for each of the people in your stories, including yourself. Close your eyes and picture each person. What details can you add to make the people in your story more real?

Describe the physical characteristics

Approximate height and weight: _____

_____

Body shape and features:_____

_____

Hair style and color: _____

_____

Facial features: (Nose, color of eyes, smile, wrinkles.)

_____

Skin: Color? Freckles? Rough? Smooth? _____

_____

Smell and touch: Perfume? Aftershave? Rough hands?

_____

_____

_____

Gestures: Head cocked when talking? Arms at side or folded?

_____

Movements: Walks quickly or slowly? Limps? Saunters?

_____

Describe the voice and speech:

Sound of voice: High? Deep? Gravelly? _____

_____

Pronunciation of words and grammar: _____

_____

Favorite words or phrases: _____

_____

_____

_____

Describe the personality:

Attitude: Upbeat? Depressed? _____

_____

Relationship to others: Outgoing? Quiet?

_____

Conversation skills: Storyteller? Listener?

_____

_____

EXERCISE
SUMMARIZE DESCRIPTIONS

When you finish filling out a worksheet for each person in your memoir, summarize your descriptions by writing five details about each person. Select the specific images that reveal the most meaningful information for each. Think about using all your senses for your descriptions.

When you complete your lists, reread your story and see if you can enhance your descriptions of the people there by adding a few significant details.

EXAMPLE

My brother Joe:
- ❏ pulled his right ear lobe when talking seriously
- ❏ face turned red when he was angry
- ❏ closet smelled like dirty socks
- ❏ snorted when he laughed hard
- ❏ smiled often

REVEAL MOTIVATIONS THROUGH ACTION

We've all heard the old adage that actions speak louder than words. In your writing, too, the activities of the people in your stories will speak loudly about them. How do you let us see the actions of the people in your stories?

Show people in action rather than *tell* us what they did. When you show people in action, we can "see" them clearly. When you tell how people acted, we don't receive a full picture.

In the following example, a writer tells about an action:

> After I told him, John just seemed to be in his own world for a while. Then he walked away.

The next example shows us the action:

> After I told him, John took a long drag on his cigarette and stared off in the distance with a scowl on his face. Then, without looking at me again, he flicked his cigarette into the bushes and strode away.

Which version reveals more about John?

Good stories center around people who want something but can't get it, as we discussed in the last step. In your writing, you need to show us what you wanted and also what you think the other people in your story wanted. Use the actions of the people in your stories to let us see their yearnings and conflicts. When a writer skillfully shows a person's actions, the motives will be exposed. Readers will see that person as a complex individual and will view those actions with understanding.

Before you write a scene, picture each person in action. Were there tears? Did someone shift weight from one foot to the other? Stomp around and yell? Cough nervously when talking?

EXERCISE
SHOW PEOPLE IN ACTION

Go back over one of your first-draft stories. Did you show people moving and reacting or did you tell us about their actions? Do you think you revealed the motivations of the people through their actions?

CREATE DIALOGUE

People become more authentic when you insert dialogue into a scene. Dialogue refers to the words people say out loud to each other, not to their interior thoughts. When you allow the people in your stories to speak, you reveal the qualities you once saw in them.

Suppose you are writing about the time your dad said you couldn't drive his car anymore. You could write: *Dad looked angry. He said he didn't trust me and took away the car keys.*

A more powerful way to recreate the scene would be to give Dad a voice:

Dad ripped the car keys out of my hand. "Mary saw you at the drive-in with seven kids in the car," he said. "I can't trust you anymore."

"But I was careful," I said.

He turned away. "You're grounded."

Of course you may not remember exactly what Dad said all those years ago, but you probably remember the scene clearly enough to recall the intent of the words that were spoken. It's OK to reinvent dialogue to give your story more immediacy, as long as you honestly choose the words you put in another person's mouth. You need to make sure those words reflect their original purpose and intention. To recreate the scenes as genuinely and truthfully as you can, try to remain true to the meaning behind the words. Use appropriate phrases that the person would have spoken in that situation.

Through the use of dialogue, a writer shows how a person thinks and reacts to situations. The spoken word reveals motivations and personalities. Your characters will come alive on the page if you allow them to speak their minds.

Tips for Writing Dialogue

❑ People usually speak in short sentences or phrases rather than in long paragraphs that give explanations. Keep the conversations concise.

❑ Put words in a speaker's mouth that move the story ahead and reveal something new about that person. Avoid pointless conversation. Readers will grow bored with dialogue such as the following: "Hi Adam, how are you?" "Oh, I'm fine, how about you?" This exchange doesn't advance the plot of your story.

❑ People often are inarticulate or vague. They use contractions and colloquial language or slang. For example, most people will say, "I don't want to go," rather than "I do not want to attend." The latter is too formal.

❑ Avoid writing dialect. When trying to recreate how a person spoke, don't try to capture an unusual dialect or a heavy accent. Readers will stumble over strange words and perhaps misunderstand the meaning of the speech.

❑ Start a new paragraph for each speaker. This helps the reader keep track of who is speaking. With separate paragraphs, you don't have to use the dialogue tags, "He said" or "she said" each time a person speaks. However, you should place dialogue tags in the first sentence of the dialogue, so a reader won't be kept guessing about who is speaking. For example:

> "I don't know what you're talking about," Harold said.
>
> "Yes, you do." Alison gave him a sideways glance.
>
> "No, really, I don't."

❏ Place all punctuation (commas, periods, question marks, etc.) inside the quotes.

❏ Use the word "said" as a dialogue tag most of the time. The word "said," used in "he said" or "I said," becomes invisible to most readers. Do not use other words each time for variety such as, "he replied," or "Mary yelled." When you use words other than "said," you interrupt the dialogue and call attention to those words. You want the reader to be absorbed in the conversation itself rather than in your description of the way the conversation is spoken.

❏ Write the person's name first, followed by the word "said." For example, write: "Bill said," rather than "said Bill."

❏ Show how someone feels through their spoken words rather than your explanation of how they felt. Consider this example:

> "I hate you," he said angrily.

The word "angrily" is not necessary. Readers can tell from the speaker's words that he is angry.

❏ Use "beats"—short phrases of action interspersed into the dialogue—to give the reader additional information about the speaker. For example, you may interrupt the dialogue with a beat to describe your friend running her hand through her long dark hair, picking some lint off her wool jacket, or stealing a glance at you. Don't overdo the use of beats, though. Readers don't like to be interrupted often.

❏ Don't use dialogue to give expository information. It will sound phony and strained. For example:

> "I baked these cookies to take to your dad's Aunt Kitty who lived in London once and moved to Pasadena thirty years ago."

If all this information about Aunt Kitty is important, reveal it to the reader in another way, not in the dialogue.

Exercise
Insert Dialogue

Look over your story and see if there is a place where you can insert some dialogue. Write out an exchange of words and then read it aloud. If possible, read it aloud to a trusted friend, or have that friend read the part of one of the people who is speaking to you, like reading a script. Listen to the way it sounds. Make changes if you need to. For more help, notice how other writers create dialogue in the books you read. Study their techniques and practice.

Take the High Road

Writing about family and close friends can be fraught with emotion and pitfalls. The greatest concern for many memoir writers is that the people they write about will be resentful or angry. How will they react to what I have to say? Will I hurt feelings or bruise egos? What if they never speak to me again? What if I create a rift in the family? What if they sue me?

The best way to handle this is to summon your larger, most compassionate self. You must be honest and tell the truth about the events you experienced, but you don't have to be mean-spirited. Think about how you would like to be remembered and offer the same fairness to the people in your stories.

The American author Napoleon Hill expressed this thought well: "If you must speak ill of another, do not speak it, write it in the sand near the water's edge."

Write with the best of intentions, with all the integrity you can bring to it. When you write a difficult scene that involves another person, it gives you the opportunity to take the high road now, even though you didn't understand the other person at the time when your story takes place. Write about how you saw the scene and be gentle with your accusations, rather than point fingers and place blame. Show how generous you can be, while still explaining how you saw the events. Then your story will have universal appeal and readers will identify with you. We all want to read about magnanimous people so we can learn how to be that way ourselves. Show us your insights. Reveal what you understand now that you didn't see then. Write about the incident showing both points of view so we can appreciate how complex it was.

"I suppose my mother was trying to be protective of me when she refused to let me drive to Cleveland with Charlie to attend Sylvia's wedding. From her perspective, as a woman who came of age in the 1930s, I see now that she just couldn't let her daughter do that. Boy, was I angry though, and worried that I would lose Charlie in the process. I wish she had handled it differently, but then, I wish I had too."

OTHER WAYS TO WRITE WITH SENSITIVITY

❑ Show your story to a family member and ask for his or her approval. If you plan to publish your memoir or distribute printed copies widely, this may be necessary to avoid invading another person's privacy. Be aware, though, that the other person may deny your request.

❑ Wait to write a story until the person who may be offended is dead. Then write the truth as you remember it, with generosity, and you will describe that individual with a clear conscience.

❑ Fictionalize elements of the story so that the truth can be told but the person cannot be recognized.

❑ Write what you can and skip the difficult, controversial parts that might ruin a relationship or cause hard feelings.

❑ Write your story as a letter to another person. You may mail it if you wish, or not. You may tear it up afterwards. If the person is no longer living and you have unfinished business that needs to come out, write the letter anyway.

However you decide to write about the people in your life, always remember that you have the right to tell your story. Don't value the opinions of someone else more than you value your own. You honor yourself by telling your story, as clearly and honestly as you can.

Always be aware, too, that our memories are not infallible. It is hard for anyone to remember events exactly as they happened. If you asked all the people in your stories to tell how they remember the events, you would find that they each recall different versions of what took place. There never is one correct version. All you can do is write your stories as you remember them, with the best of intentions.

You are not a journalist, but you should strive to tell the truth as you experienced it. You cannot be an impartial writer of events, because you reside at the heart of your stories, with all your thoughts and emotions. Treat others in your story with understanding, whether it is through your feelings at the time or your more mature insights now. When you connect to a person's humanity, no matter what your relationship, your readers will connect with you.

WHAT IF IT'S TOO DIFFICULT?

If you can't write a scene right now because of the deep emotions involved, you have several options.

❑ Don't write about it at this time. Maybe it's too soon. Don't force it. You will know when you are ready to write about it.

❑ Write about a difficult personal relationship but don't include that scene in your book. Put it in a safe place and read it at a later time. You may decide to rewrite it or edit what you have written. You may decide to tear it up. It's your decision.

❑ Write the story from the perspective of the third person, using "he" or "she" to refer to yourself. Later you may decide to write it again from your point of view.

❑ Write a difficult scene that you were a part of, from the other person's point of view. Consider why the person behaved that way. Describe your reactions in the scene from that person's point of view. Put your story away for a few days or weeks. Go back and write the scene again from your point of view. Have you gained any insights that you can add? Is it a richer and more complex story now?

SHOULD I AIR ALL MY DIRTY LAUNDRY?

It's a good idea to think clearly about what you want to leave behind. Do your heirs need to know about that love affair? Do they need to know about your abortion? Will this open up deep wounds? Will it cause unnecessary anger and angst? If you like to stir things up, proceed. But think about it. There are some things you may just have to write about for yourself, perhaps in a private journal where you can get it off your chest. Then decide later if you want it to become a part of the memoir you leave behind for others to read about your life.

Consider your audience. If you're writing a book to sell to a general audience, the more you reveal honestly, the more the readers will identify with you and want to buy your book. If you're writing strictly for your family, though, you may want to hold back the most awkward details.

TIPS

❑ Tell the truth about people as you remember it.

❑ Write vividly about people by using sensory details to describe them, action scenes that show motivation, and dialogue.

❑ Be compassionate rather than mean-spirited when writing about others.

❑ Remember you have the right to tell your story.

BEFORE YOU GO ON TO THE NEXT STEP

Go back through all the stories you have written so far. Did you accurately describe the people in your stories by using sensory details? Did you show them in action? Did you insert dialogue to give them voice? Try to inject fairness and compassion into the way you portray others. Then go on to the next step to learn about finding meaning in your stories.

SHOW AND TELL

She smiled at me when I entered; a quick eye-squeeze of recognition, then the blank look returned. She had no idea who I was. After 30 years of being married to her son, weekly visits and phone calls, countless family dinners with her and our children, I was a stranger to her. I held her hand and stroked her arm as she smiled at me. She knew I was someone kind. Perhaps she could see that I loved her so.

She covered her forgetfulness with smiles and social skills that still prevailed. She used to have opinions about politics, theater and recent films, but now it was as though the curtain had fallen on her stage and the lights had dimmed forever. I tried not to let her see my teary eyes. She focused on our hands together and then the light at the window, as I chatted on about the kids' families and the neighbor's crazy cat. The talk was inconsequential, but I was there. How I missed the person she was.

Step 8

Look for Meaning in What you Write

> "All truths are easy to understand
> once they are discovered;
> the point is to discover them."
> —Galileo Galilei

As you write about your life, you will find yourself probing deeper to discover the meaning hidden there. You will discover that every experience has been a teacher. Writing about these experiences will start a process of learning and growth. Each story you write will give you new insights.

Your memoir will give you back your past, with all its difficult encounters and positive adventures. Subconscious thoughts will burst through your writing. When you complete your book, you will be able to look back over the whole to see themes or patterns you missed before. Writing will give you the perspective to rediscover the reasons for doing what you did.

You also will become aware that events seldom happened in a linear fashion that led to neat conclusions. You will see that when you started moving in one direction, something often happened to divert your attention. You finally landed that dream job and then your spouse was transferred to another state. You signed up to take a long-awaited painting class just when someone close to you became ill and needed your help. You moved your office into your grown son's old bedroom and then he moved back home to get on his feet again. What insights did you learn along the way?

Writing can provide a way to make sense of this chaos. The very process of writing helps you organize your thoughts and sort out the jumble of happenings around you. It tames the mental circus that plays in your brain. Once you've transferred muddled thoughts from your mind onto the page or a computer screen, you will be cognizant of new perceptions and awareness.

Like an insect captured in amber, the meaning of your experiences will remain stuck in your memory until you extract it and examine it close up. Writing will focus your vision so you can see what lies buried inside.

The understanding is already inside you. Your writing will instruct you. You will grow emotionally as you revisit your experiences. All you need to do is keep writing and trust the process.

SHOW AND TELL

Fiction writers are encouraged to "show," not "tell." In other words, they need to dramatize scenes by adding action and dialogue to "show" the motivations of the characters and the arc of the story. This makes the story come alive more than "telling" it, which can be dull and passive. In Step 7, I suggested that you borrow this tool of fiction writers to "show" the actions of the people in your stories, rather than tell about what they did.

Yet writing a memoir, which is a true story of your experiences, is different from writing fiction. Good memoir writers both "show" AND "tell." That means you need to "show" the action and also "tell" how those events shaped you.

This is the main reason we write about our lives—to discover meaning. It is also the main reason others will want to read about your life.

When you reflect on events and open your eyes to the new perspectives to be found there, you will encounter the wisdom of your truths. Without those revelations, your story will be empty. It will leave both you and your reader with a shallow experience, wondering about your awareness. You've only dipped your toe into the water, but you haven't bathed in new understanding. You've stated the facts, but found no meaning.

While you may be more comfortable narrating from a distant shore, now is the time to jump into your story and "show" the action. Then "tell" us how these events impacted your life.

In *The Writer and her Work*, the well-known author Joan Didion tells us, "I write entirely to find out what I'm thinking, what I'm looking at, what I see and what it means. What I want and what I fear." Like Didion, you can use your writing to reflect on your life. It will help you grow as a writer and as a human being.

Your writing will be best when it ventures close to a nerve, like a dentist drilling in a molar without Novocaine. When you feel an uncomfortable twinge, that's where the story is most interesting. From there, you can glimpse emotional truths with more clarity. Use those razor-sharp insights to write honestly. If you skirt around them, your writing will be dull and predictable. Your reader will sense your arms going up into a fold across your chest. "Yes," you are saying, "I had this experience, but I'm not inviting you in to see how I actually felt about it."

Be aware, as you write, of this need to connect authentically with your readers. Let them know how you felt about the action taking place around you. Show how you filtered the events in your story. Tell about what made you angry and what made you laugh. Write about how you dealt with difficult situations. Describe how your experiences moved you or hardened you. Take time to reflect. Then as you write, think about how you can both show the action and tell about the meaning you have discovered.

EXERCISE
TELL HOW YOU FELT

Reread one of the stories you have written. Did you reflect on your feelings about the major events you described? If not, go back now and tell how you felt about these experiences—both how you felt about them then and how you feel about them now in retrospect.

How Can I Uncover My Truth?

Memoir is about telling the truth as you see it. It's about disclosing what is in your heart and uncovering the face behind the mask. As a memoirist, you try as honestly as you can to recreate experiences that happened some time ago, from your perspective. And in the writing of those stories, you try to find meaning and deeper understanding.

The best way to uncover your emotional truths is to write your story first and then go back to write some more. Hover your pen over the paper or your fingers above the keyboard. Now drill a little deeper. Ask yourself questions about your story. How did I get to that place? Why did I make that decision? Where did it lead me? Was it the right choice? How did I feel about it then? What can I honestly say about the situation now?

A story comes to life when you marry the facts with your emotional truth. For example, when you write about how your mother died just after you walked into the hospital room, tell about the scene from your point of view. It was her death, but you need to write about how it affected you as you arrived at her bedside just when she took her last breath.

Another way to reveal emotional truths is to show your humanity, with all its foibles. Write about your mistakes and your most embarrassing moments. Good public speakers tell self-effacing stories about themselves to endear them to their audiences. They call it "leveling." See if you can do some leveling in your memoir. Your readers will see you as a real person they can relate to and they will love you.

So tell about the time you came out of a pub restroom in Hamburg and walked down the street with a long stream of toilet paper stuck to your heel. Admit to the time when you pretended not to see your father at the high school football game because you were suddenly embarrassed by how old he looked compared to the other boy's dads. Tell us about when you flirted openly with your best friend's date at the senior prom just because you knew you looked good.

With memoir, readers want to have the sense that they are reading something authentic. They want the truth. This is the unspoken contract between a memoir writer and a reader. Your audience wants to make a connection with you through your honest portrayal of your experiences and the emotions you felt. They want to trust you. They want to learn something that is valid and real.

EXERCISE

REWRITE AND REVEAL MORE

Look back over one of your stories to see if you can rewrite it to reveal your emotional truth. When you write about that fight you had with your sister, see if you can identify new understandings to replace the untidy grudges you first reported. If the incident happened in a kitchen, go to the kitchen to write. Listen to some music from that time. Reimagine it. What do you see? What do you feel?

Your Search for Meaning

Writing your memoir can change your life. Ask anyone who has completed a memoir and you will hear stories about cleansing old wounds, gaining deeper understanding, and increasing confidence. Health professionals also tout the benefits of writing a personal narrative.

Dr. James Pennebaker, a social psychologist from the University of Texas, Austin, has published extensive research about the power of writing to heal. His research has shown that the act of writing about life experiences and searching for their meaning can improve mental health. Pennebaker published a seminal paper about the health benefits of writing about life in the *Journal of Clinical Psychology* in 1999.

That article gave scientific weight to what the writing community had known: writing a narrative of your life that includes not only what happened, but also your feelings about it, provides long-term positive psychological effects.

Pennebaker showed that writing about emotional experiences releases pent-up tensions and allows the writer to move toward a new way of living. As words wash over the page, anger and other negative emotions begin to disappear.

Talking about life events doesn't give as deep an understanding as writing about them, although talking is the main tool used by psychologists. When we speak our stories out loud, we release emotions that uncover the truth. Yet the spoken word is ephemeral, and soon disappears into the shifty clouds of memory. The written word, on the other hand, exists on paper or electronically, where it can be reread and examined.

Writing about our lives allows us to create a structure to organize the seeming randomness of our experiences. It gives us the opportunity to come face-to-face with events again and to understand what happened. We can read and re-read our stories. We can write and rewrite them. In a sense, we can become the authors of our lives. Once we observe the general plot line and focus on how we responded to past events, we gain the confidence to envision what we will do in the future.

Pennebaker conducted studies about writing and its relation to physical health as well. Astonishingly, he found that writing about your life relieves stress so well, it actually boosts the immune system. Pennebaker also has proven that writing can lessen the severity of many illnesses, including arthritis, asthma, and heart disease. And, he says, when you share your writing with others you trust, the benefits compound.

EXERCISE
DIG DEEPER

Look back at one of the stories you wrote. Pay attention to the times your emotions poked through. When you wrote something like, "I was worried," or "I was angry," take note and try to go deeper there. You are expressing something that is on the surface. To find out what is below that statement, put your pen on the paper and explore why you expressed those feelings. Ask yourself, "Why was I so worried then?" Or "Why was I so angry?" See what you can learn.

AVOIDING THE TRUTH

You may not be ready to write about your mother so soon after she died. Or you may have buried your sorrow about a former marriage so deep that you can't face dredging it up yet. Touching that raw spot may be uncomfortable and frightening. Often we try to avoid the truth by writing around it or ignoring the elephant on the page. Our truth can be frightening to confront. Sometimes we just don't want to write about it.

If you aren't able to write about an emotional experience right now, don't force yourself. Write about other parts of your life and revisit this idea later. Your success in writing about more positive aspects of your life eventually will encourage you to write about the difficult ones. You also may find some relief in talking to a professional to help unlock your past before you try to write about it.

Yet don't abandon that difficult story forever. When you encounter resistance in your writing, it usually means you have found the very story you need to write. Do you race through the writing of difficult events? Are you using generalities rather than telling a story with specific details? You may be avoiding your emotional truth there.

When you do feel ready to write the story that has been festering in your brain, let it come out without thinking about it or revising it. Just let it roll out onto the page. Then put it away and read what you wrote at another time. You may be surprised by its fury. It may be perfect as it is, in its raw power. Or you may want to write it again, with dialogue and more details. You can write about it as many times as you want.

Eventually, you will absorb its full meaning. When you finally write about the truth of your experience, you will start to heal and move on with your life.

EXERCISE
WRITE WITH THE THIRD PERSON

Write about something that you have been avoiding. To make it easier, try telling the story using the third person ("he" or "she") when you refer to yourself. Later, rewrite it in the first person, from your point of view, using "I." Add your feelings about the events.

LINK YOUR STORY TO HISTORY

If you want to ensure that people will find your memoir meaningful well after you are gone, make your story larger than you are. Place yourself in the historical and cultural context of your lifetime. Shift your view from the microscope that sees details, to a wide-angle lens. How does your life fit into the bigger picture of what was going on in the world around you?

See if you can find some intersections between your experiences and well-known people or historical events. Did a famous sports figure go to your high school? Did you shake the president's hand when he campaigned in your town? What was your connection to Vietnam during the war? Perhaps your father's cousin worked on the first lunar landing in 1969 and invited your family to Florida to see the launch? Maybe your best friend had polio back when there was no vaccine? Perhaps you traveled to Iran before the Shah was deposed? Or you took part in a march for the ERA or played a part in the Civil Rights movement? Your connections to well-known people and important events will add depth to your memoir.

Even if you didn't participate in events that you consider to be newsworthy, perhaps some happenings influenced you from afar? None of us lives in a vacuum. Our private experiences often reflect what is happening in the broader society. Do some research about the political and social issues of the years since your birth, and see if any of them connect with your life. Did you obtain a scholarship because of affirmative action? Did you miss a promotion to the job you really wanted because you are a woman? Were your travels interrupted because of international events?

Link your story to history and it becomes a broader, more fascinating story. Your readers will have a hook to identify with you. By enlarging the context of your story, you may be able to explain why you did what you did while living in those times.

WORKSHEET
Discover Historical Context

Use the following worksheet to place yourself into the historical context of your life. What did these events mean to you? How did they shape you? Write a few notes about each of the questions here and then see if you can weave some of these events into your stories.

The Women's Movement: changing professional opportunities, social and sexual freedoms, the Pill, the Glass Ceiling, continuing discrimination

———————————————————————————

———————————————————————————

Racial and cultural experiences: discrimination, breaking barriers, new professional opportunities, acceptance, overt and underlying tensions

———————————————————————————

———————————————————————————

Historic and political events that affected you: September 11, 2001, presidential assassinations, wars, elections

———————————————————————————

Natural disasters you lived through: earthquakes, hurricanes, wildfires, floods

———————————————————————————

Famous people you met or had a connection to

_____

_____

Favorite music, books, plays, art that influenced you

_____

_____

Important and well-known events you witnessed: Inaugura-
tion, rocket launch, funeral of an important person, Mardi
Gras, the Olympics

_____

_____

Religious and spiritual connections you made

_____

_____

Places you visited at significant times

_____

_____

Organizations you participated in that shaped your world

_____

_____

_____

_____

Do I Need a Theme?

Go back and reread all the stories you have written. Do you see a theme that runs through these collected stories? Are you beginning to discover a unified thread that may hint at why you are writing your memoir?

A real story can be more compelling than fiction. Yet, like a novelist, you need to present the arc of your life experiences. Show how you went from confusion to a greater understanding. See if you can discover the values that underlie your actions. The more you can show the universality of your experiences and the humanity of the people you write about, the more your story will resonate with others.

Readers are hungry to learn something universal. They want to identify with you and apply your lessons to their lives. Look for universal themes that reveal themselves in your stories. Perhaps at the core of all your stories is your struggle to balance work and family. Or maybe you dealt with a sense of loss for many years after your parents separated. When you tap into a theme that is larger than your life experience, you will create a powerful story.

You may find at first that you have the beginnings of several different memoirs rather than one account with a unifying theme. Your memoir may be a collection of unrelated stories that reflect the variety of your life experiences.

Yet when a theme shines through all of your stories, you can begin to see how your book will be organized. While you will want to include all the stories you write, some may not make the cut, if they don't illustrate your theme. You also may see that you need to reorder your stories, even if your new order doesn't exactly follow the chronology of the events. Once you have a clearer idea of what it is that you're are writing about, you will see the path you need to take to complete your memoir.

It may take some time to tease out the meaning of the stories you have written about the trajectory of your life. It's right there in front of you, but you may not be ready to see it until you have written more. Eventually, though, a theme with new understandings will emerge from your narrative.

Exercise
Find a Theme

Review the stories you have written and try to find a common thread. What are you saying in all these stories? Is there a theme? Is your memoir about finding yourself? Or your struggles? Or your faith? What is it that you are saying, over and over? Which stories fit with that theme? Which ones can be eliminated from your final memoir?

Tips

❑ Reread all your stories. Did you show *and* tell?

❑ Ask yourself—what is my book about? What is its meaning? What do I want others to understand about me from reading my book?

❑ Write down the one truth you know about your life. Is this the theme of your memoir?

❑ If you have trouble writing about emotional events, wait until you are ready.

Before you go on to the next step

Keep writing until you have finished telling all of your stories for this memoir. With each chapter, write a first draft and then rewrite the stories, where appropriate, using what you learned in Steps 6–8. Did you add specific stories with structure? Did you write carefully about the people in your life and write honestly about yourself? Did you place your narrative into a larger context rooted in history and universal values? As you continue to write about your life, you will experience the healing value of seeing beyond what you could see before. That new vision will help you identify a theme and the broader meaning of your life experiences.

In the next step you will learn how to make final revisions to your manuscript and prepare it for printing. You are nearly finished. Keep going until you are satisfied that you have told the whole story. Your memoir will be a priceless gift for others, filled with compelling narratives of your experiences and your truths.

REVISION

We wandered into the courtyard through a carved wooden gate. Inside, a woman ~~was peering~~ *peered* out at us from behind a ragged shawl and ~~was pointing~~ *pointed* at our feet. She wanted us to remove our shoes and place them in a pile. My white sandals stood out against the rubber flip flops that ~~were~~ heaped beside the entrance.

The courtyard bricks ~~were very hot on~~ *burned* our bare feet as we ~~walked quickly~~ *scurried* across to the shade of the temple. On the lattice wall ~~were~~ *we noticed* yellow ribbons fluttering in the breeze. A turbaned man ~~was leaning~~ *leaned* against the wall, ~~holding~~ *fingering* his worry beads. When he saw us he waved a fistful of yellow ribbons and called out to me. "Do you want a boy?"

"Pardon me?" I ~~shouted as I~~ moved closer.

"If you want to have a boy, take a yellow ribbon and tie it on the wall," he said. "If you want a girl, take a green one."

STEP 9

REVISE YOUR MANUSCRIPT

"WRITING IS A TWO-STEP PROCESS:
THROW UP AND CLEAN UP."
—Ray Bradbury (personal communication)

WRITE FIRST, REVISE SECOND

This step will be useful to you once you have completed writing drafts of all the stories for your memoir. Those first drafts are the "throw-up" phase—that is, getting your stories down on paper. During this process you made some changes too, with Steps 6, 7, and 8, which led you to add story structure, dialogue, and personal reflections. This step will involve a final "clean up." Now you will revise your memoir as a whole to prepare it for final printing.

"Revision" means to "see again." This step provides the opportunity to revise your entire memoir, to make sure the chapters cover your significant experiences and flow together in a logical order. This step also will give you suggestions for a revision of word usage—verbs, adverbs, and adjectives, in particular—so your stories will say precisely what you want them to say.

Think of yourself as a gardener. You planted your garden with seeds some months ago. Over time, the seeds grew into young plants. Now you need to weed out the small or weak plants and fertilize the strongest so they can mature and blossom. Remember that it's your garden. You are the planter and the pruner. You are the one to determine how it will achieve its eventual form and beauty.

Start Revision with the Big Picture

Open your three-ring Memoir Notebook and reread all the stories you have written. Try to reread it all in one sitting. Is there an obvious theme to your memoir? See if you can group all the stories you have written under one working title, such as, "My Teaching Career," or "Our Family," or "Traveling the World," or "My Battle with Cancer."

As you reread your manuscript, ask yourself what the purpose is for each scene. Does it explain how you felt about that part of your life? Perhaps you now see the need to add a scene or two, to fill in the unexplained parts of a long narrative and reinforce your theme.

Maybe you will discover some scenes that don't fit. The choice to leave out a story you have already written can be difficult, but if it doesn't support the topic of your memoir, it may need to be dropped. You can't chronicle everything. It's as important to decide what to take out as to determine what to leave in.

Ask yourself what stories excite you. Which ones sizzle on the page? What parts seem dull? If they bore you, they probably will bore your readers too. Throw out the weaker stories or rework them.

❑ Do my stories appear in the book in a logical order? Do I need to change the order so there is an understandable progression to the narrative, even if the stories don't follow the chronological order in which they happened?

❑ Are the different parts of my memoir linked together with transitions so the reader can see how one event led to another?

❑ Does my entire memoir have a beginning, middle, and end that shows the arc of how I grew and changed?

❑ Did I adequately explain who all the people are in my stories so that readers in the future will understand their connection to me?

Consider the preceding list while you reread your entire manuscript. Make comments in the margins as you read through all your stories. Mark the confusing places that need more explanation. Look for places where you need to add a paragraph that links two ideas. Highlight the scenes that may not be necessary to tell your story and note the places that beg you to write another scene. See if you need to change the order of your stories.

Narrow Your Focus

Once you have completed a broad review of your memoir, it's time to look at your writing through a narrower lens. Now you will look at sentence construction and word usage to revise your manuscript, line by line. Have you written the same words over and over? Did you add enough sensory details? Did you use incomplete or run-on sentences? Does your writing engage the reader because the sentences use the active voice? Did you use strong, descriptive verbs?

Writing is a craft that you learn by paying attention and practicing. You can find many excellent books that will teach you to write better prose. Some of them are listed in the Suggested Readings section at the end of this book, and I recommend you read some of them if you wish to be become a better writer.

If you compose your manuscript on a computer, you can use the correction programs in your word-processing software to edit your work for grammar, punctuation, and spelling or typos. Yet you can't rely on software for all your revisions. You need to proofread carefully to make the corrections that only you can make, such as the exact names for distant relatives and the correct spelling of the names of the streets and towns you mention.

I also suggest you have an editor or a writer friend review your manuscript and proofread it for basic grammar and punctuation errors. This person also may have some broader suggestions for editing the intent and meaning of your stories. It's up to you to decide if you want to accept these suggestions.

You may want to gather several opinions from trusted friends and colleagues.

I could give you so many suggestions as you revise your manuscript, but this book is about writing memoir, so I'll just offer three basic writing suggestions that I think will help make your writing sparkle:

1. Use strong, powerful verbs and few adverbs.
2. Use the active voice.
3. Use colorful and precise descriptive words.

On the next few pages you will find each of these suggestions explained. Read through the explanations and work on the exercises. Then go back through your manuscript one last time to see where you can exchange dull verbs with exciting ones and make your writing sing by switching to the active voice and adding evocative adjectives.

REVISION TIP: USE STRONG VERBS

Verbs create the action in your story. Good writers use engaging, robust verbs to evoke clear pictures in the minds of their readers. For example, think about the different images you see if, instead of the word "walk," you substitute verbs such as "trudge," "dawdle," "tiptoe," "prowl," or "amble." Each of these verbs conveys a vivid image of how a person walks.

Weak verbs such as "is," "was," "are," "have," "had," and "seem" slow down the story and take the energy out of your writing.

Note: Sometimes these weak verbs are necessary to convey your meaning (as in this sentence, which uses "are.") Use them sparingly however. You won't engage a reader if you rely on weak verbs throughout your writing.

Some suggestions to help you write with strong, descriptive verbs:

❏ Imagine the action of your scene as clearly as you can and then write down a list of verbs to describe the activities you "see." For example, if you describe how you ice skated when you were a child, you may write down verbs such as: "spin," "twirl," "race," "swoop," and "wobble." Refer to that list while you revise your story.

❏ Use a thesaurus or a dictionary for inspiration.

❏ Write your story first, then go back and circle all the verbs you wrote. Take out as many of the forms of the "to be" verb (is, are, was, were) as possible. Substitute lively, rich verbs.

❏ Start noticing verbs in the books you read. Identify which verbs enhance the writing you enjoy. Make a list of the powerful verbs used by good writers and try to use them in your own writing.

Exercise
Replace Weak Verbs

❑ Read the following paragraph. Highlight or circle the weak verbs, such as "was," "were," and "seemed." Think of better verbs to replace them and rewrite the paragraph below. Try to visualize how the dog looked when he played with the Frisbee.

"Our dog, Pepper, was black and his ears were very long. He was always shedding his thick black hair in the summer when he was hot. His favorite game was playing catch with a Frisbee. When he was young he could catch it, but when he was old, he was too slow. The times he seemed most happy were when he had that Frisbee in his mouth. He would chew on it until he was tired. We would give him a bone to chew on sometimes, but he didn't seem to want it. He was happier with the Frisbee."

Hint: shedded, flopped, leapt, hung, loved, gnawed, caught, slowed, exhausted, bounded, and rejected

AVOID ADVERBS

Writers sometimes use adverbs in place of strong verbs. Adverbs modify or explain the meaning of verbs and adjectives. Most adverbs end in "ly," such as "suddenly," "sadly," "noisily," "gratefully," or "slowly." Other popular adverbs are "very" and "quite."

While adverbs can be necessary to convey the exact meaning of some sentences, they lose their punch when they are overused. Some writers use them as crutches to strengthen weak verbs. If you want to improve your writing, try to eliminate your use of adverbs. Instead, find an appropriate verb without an adverb to create a precise image.

WEAK WRITING WITH A VERB AND AN ADVERB	BETTER WRITING WITH A STRONG VERB
He walked slowly.	He sauntered. Or: He plodded.
She spoke loudly.	She shouted.
She fit tightly into the seat.	She squeezed into the seat.

EXERCISE

REWRITE ADVERB PHRASES

The sentences below use an adverb to explain the full meaning of the verb. Rewrite the sentences with strong verbs that eliminate the need for the adverbs.

He pushed her roughly.

The boy rode by quickly on his bike.

He spoke softly.

He drove very fast.

She said it suddenly.

Hint: shoved, sped, muttered, raced, or blurted. Can you think of others?

Now look at your own writing. Can you replace adverb phrases with strong verbs?

Revision Tip: Use the Active Voice

A verb has an active voice when the subject of the sentence performs the action. For example: "Native Americans painted art on these rocks long ago."

A verb has a passive voice when the action is performed on the subject. For example: "Art was painted by Native Americans on these rocks long ago." Writers use passive voice when they don't want to state the subject or when they don't know it. For example: "Art was painted on these rocks long ago."

Active voice is direct, clear, and concise. The reader knows who performed the action. Active voice creates visual images in the mind of the reader. The passive voice adds unnecessary words (such as "was") to a sentence that slows the reader down. If readers don't know who completed the action, they won't create clear mental images of the action.

Scholars and business writers use passive voice. An example of that same sentence in the passive voice would be: "Passive voice is used in scholarly or business writing." Do you see the difference?

Some writers think their writing will sound more polished or impressive if they use passive voice. They may write passive-voice sentences without even realizing it. Yet, passive voice distances the reader from the writer and makes for slow, boring reading. Readers tune out when they have to plow through a lot of this kind of writing. For your memoir, make it clear in your sentences who is performing the action. To do this, use the active voice most of the time.

EXERCISE
IDENTIFY PASSIVE VOICE

Practice identifying passive voice by studying the sentences below. Rewrite each sentence in active voice:

A poem was written by Mary.

The boat was driven by Dad.

Some debates were won by our team.

EXERCISE
ACTIVATE YOUR PASSIVE VOICE

As you revise your own manuscript, cross out and rewrite sentences that are written in the passive voice. (The second part of that sentence uses passive voice. Did you catch it?) To say the same thing in active voice: "As you revise your manuscript, cross out and rewrite the sentences you wrote in the passive voice."

REVISION TIP: CAPTURE IMAGES
WITH PRECISE ADJECTIVES

When you recreate scenes from your past, you need to select precise adjectives to describe the scenes and people. You already completed a series of exercises in Step 4 that tapped your memory for sensory details. Most of those details are "adjectives"—words that modify or explain the nouns in your sentences. I asked you then to revisit the memories provided by your senses (sight, sound, smell, taste, and touch) to recall details before you wrote each of your stories.

For example, if you wrote about your childhood home, I suggested you use your senses to add telling details, such as the cabinets' chipped turquoise paint, the stuffy smell in the attic bedroom, the creak of the stairs and how the cold linoleum floor felt on your bare feet. The adjectives in that sentence are: chipped, turquoise, stuffy, creak, cold, linoleum, and bare. These adjectives give precise descriptions of the cabinets, attic, stairs, floor, and feet. Readers can picture the scene exactly when these descriptions are used.

As you reread your stories, think about your use of descriptive adjectives once more. Make sure your adjectives convey clear images. Good writers use precise adjectives rather than tired and ambiguous words such as "beautiful," "wonderful," and "big." These words are vague and can mean different things to different people. Consider the word "beautiful," for example. Your idea of what is beautiful may be very different from mine. Beauty truly is in the eye of the beholder. Before you use a generic adjective such as "beautiful," ask yourself what it means to you. Search for the exact word to convey your meaning. You may want to use a thesaurus.

EXERCISE
REPLACE OVERUSED ADJECTIVES

In the following examples, try your hand at replacing the overused adjective "beautiful" with more precise words. Ask yourself what the word "beautiful" means to you in each context.

The beautiful sky   Better: The _____sky

The beautiful car   Better: The _____ car

The beautiful child   Better: The _____child

The beautiful dog   Better: The _____dog

Hint: cloudless, pink, sleek, polished, curly-haired, straight-haired, black-eyed, blue-eyed, shiny coated, long legged. Can you think of others?

A caveat: While you need to select the right details to describe a scene, don't overdo it. Too many adjectives can get in the way of the action. You will bog down your story if you introduce a scene or a person using phrases such as: "There was . . ." or "He/she had . . ." before a list of descriptions. Instead, be selective when you choose your adjectives, and only use the significant and meaningful ones.

You also can reveal descriptive details with the action of the story. For example, instead of writing, "There was a heavy screen door at the front of the house," you could include that bit of information in the action by writing, "Mother opened the heavy screen door to let me in." Or, instead of writing, "Sue had curly red hair," you could tell the same information by saying, "Sue pulled her curly red hair into a ponytail before she jumped into the pool."

FINAL SUGGESTIONS FOR YOUR REVISION:

Revise your work by yourself first.

When you revise, you must be honest with yourself and leave your ego outside the door. You need to make the hard choices about what stories to keep or remove. The process can be compared to taking an ax to a grove of trees and eliminating the dead limbs that keep out the sun.

Try reading your work out loud to hear your authentic voice. When you read your stories out loud, you will hear the obvious clunkers. Your ear will tell you faster than your eye if it sounds right. In fact, sometimes you will find yourself changing the written words when you read them out loud to make them sound better to you. Note those places and make the changes on the page.

❧❦❧

Then find an editor to help you.

If your own inner critic is too hard on you, find another person whom you trust to read your work. You need someone who will tell you which parts are excellent, which parts need to be rewritten, and which parts do not belong at all.

Many writers find that read-and-critique groups are helpful, even vital. Members of the group who hear your writing for the first time can give you honest feedback. With a large group, you may receive conflicting critique. It's up to you to decide which comments you want to use for your revisions. You may not use them all, but at least you will have a good idea of the parts that work and the parts that need to be changed. You also may want to hire a professional editor.

❧❦❧

Rewrite some scenes from scratch.

Sometimes it may be best to completely rewrite a scene, rather than edit the already-written sentences. Put the first draft aside and start over. This time, dig deeper. As you imagine the scene again, what catches your attention this time?

ల౷౦ఎ

Revise until you are satisfied.

You may wonder how many drafts you need to write. The simple answer is: as many as it takes. Some stories may need several rewrites. Others may not require much reworking at all. Most people complete at least two or three rewrites and often many more. Only you will know when you are finished and satisfied that you have told your story as well as possible.

As you revise, it's important to maintain the excitement in your writing. Keep that spark that led you to write it in the first place. So don't cut the heart out of your story when you revise it. Too much revision will extinguish your story's vitality.

Your memoir will never be perfect. There is no such thing. Work on revising it only until it feels right to you. If your goal is to complete your memoir, you will need to declare it finished at some point. Then you will be able to move to the last step and complete your book.

TIPS

❑ Write first, revise later (Throw up—Clean up).

❑ Start by revising with the big picture, then narrow your focus to the details.

❑ Read your stories out loud to hear your authentic voice.

❑ Don't revise too much—keep the fire.

WRITING PRACTICE

Read over your entire book. Write a summary of your book on one or two pages. Does it cover what you want to say? Have you left anything out? Edit it for clarity, grammar, and spelling. Then type it up and place it at the front of your three-ring Memoir Notebook. This short summary may be used as an introduction for your book, or for the section titled, "About the Author." It is written by you and contains the main points of your life in a succinct form.

BEFORE YOU GO ON TO THE NEXT STEP

Now that you have completed your book, it's time to write an introduction. You may find it amusing that I suggest you write an introduction after you have written your whole memoir. Yet that is what most authors do. When you finish the entire book, you will know what you want to say. Explain how you came to write this memoir and what you hope it will accomplish. Thank the people who helped you complete your book. Tell how you strived to be honest and fair. Explain that you wrote the stories from your point of view, and your memories may be different from the recollections of others.

When you finish your final revisions, you can turn your attentions to transforming your typed manuscript into an actual book. So, turn the page now and take the last step to becoming the author of your own memoir.

STEP 10

COMPLETE YOUR BOOK

"GREAT WORKS ARE PERFORMED NOT BY STRENGTH
BUT BY PERSEVERANCE."
—Samuel Johnson

If you have stayed with me through all the suggestions in the last 9 Steps, you have finished writing your memoir. Congratulations! That's a huge accomplishment. Your writing project has required commitment and a willingness to persevere. You have spent countless hours remembering, reflecting, and learning how to write about your life. I hope it has been a rewarding experience—perhaps even life-changing.

Now it's time to turn your attention to the final design and printing of your book. How do you want your memoir to look? Use the following checklist to make sure your book has all the necessary components and is organized the way you want it before you make plans to set it in stone.

❑ Type a fresh copy of your entire manuscript or have someone do it for you.

❑ Go through the photos you selected in Step 3 and decide where you would like to insert them in the chapters.

❑ Organize the memorabilia or the photos of memorabilia that you have gathered for your book. Plan the placement of those photos in the book.

❑ Go to a bookstore or library and look at published memoirs. What sizes, bindings and designs appeal to you?

PRINTING AND PUBLISHING YOUR BOOK

While you have been writing your book, you have given a great deal of thought to your readers. Now you need to think about how they will obtain your book so they can read it. Do you picture them walking into a book store to buy your published book off the shelf? Do you hope to have it available on Amazon? Do you want to give printed books personally to your family and friends?

Authors today face an array of options, from laying out a book on a computer and printing it at a local copy store, to selling it to a publisher that will print and market it. Your choice will be based on many factors, including the marketability of your book, the number of books you want to print, the amount of money you want to spend and how professional you want it to look.

These decisions need research and thought. Ask yourself what kind of written legacy you want to leave. You can find many books and online resources to help you make the right choice. This chapter outlines the main printing and publishing options available. I suggest you read these brief summaries and then do more research to make sure your final product will meet your expectations.

The first decision you need to make is whether you want to sell your book to a wide audience through a publisher or give your book to family and friends. You have many choices for each of these options in the changing world of book printing and publishing. Consider the following methods and decide which will work best for you.

PUBLISH AND SELL YOUR BOOK

LARGE PUBLISHERS

You, like many authors, may dream of publishing your book with a large press, such as Random House, Penguin, or HarperCollins. These publishers, mostly based in New York City, will print, advertise, and distribute a book, plus pay an advance to the author. If the book sells well, the author also will receive royalties.

That sounds great, but you must be aware that it is extremely difficult to sell a book to one of the large publishing houses. They are in the business of making money, and in a very competitive world, they can be choosy about the books they decide to publish. Your book must have a well-written, compelling story. It also helps if you are famous or have participated in a noteworthy or historic event.

Still, if this is your dream, you should pursue it. Large publishers do not accept unsolicited manuscripts, so you will need to hire a literary agent who specializes in working with memoirists and who will represent you to the publisher. You will need persistence and a well-written, timely manuscript to find an agent who is willing to work with you. Agents want to make a profit too, and they will select only those authors whose work they think they can sell to a publisher.

In summary, it's not impossible, but it is very difficult for a first-time author to sell a memoir to a big publisher.

SMALL PUBLISHERS

You may have better luck publishing your book through a small press. These independent or university presses may be interested in your book because of a local angle or your school connections. They may not offer an advance or a large royalty, but they usually will pay an author about 10 percent of the gross book price, once they have printed the book. Authors can submit book proposals to small presses on their own, or find a literary agent to help. Small presses don't have large advertising budgets, so you will need to assist with the marketing. They may not have book-store distribution networks either, but they will sell books through their websites or on other online book sources.

With both large and small publishers, authors need to be prepared to help promote their own books, through their websites or personal appearances.

SELF-PUBLISH

Computer technology has upended the rigid publishing world. While self-publishing was once looked down on as "vanity publishing," it is now an acceptable and mushrooming business. It allows thousands of authors to publish their own books without having to worry about being rejected by the big publishing house gate-keepers. Self-publishing means that you become the publisher of your book and you hire a company to print it. Companies that offer self-publishing provide a whole range of services to help authors create a book, including editing, proofing, printing, and marketing strategies. You decide which services you want to buy and you have control over the whole process.

The main advantage of self-publishing is that after you pay these upfront costs, you get to keep the sales profits. The downside is that in addition to paying to have the book printed, you need to handle the marketing and distribution of the books or pay for assistance in those areas. Most bookstores will not sell self-published books because the big publishers control the distribution networks. So you need to find other ways to sell self-published books, such as through a website, social media, or by word of mouth. Unless you hire someone to help, you will find yourself running a small business that involves marketing, filling orders, and mailing the books to customers.

Despite these difficulties, more and more authors today decide to publish their books themselves. Self-published books can sell well, if the author is diligent and clever about advertising. In fact, the market for self-published books is growing faster than the market for professionally published books. And if a book sells well, a large publisher may eventually notice and buy the rights to publish and sell the book.

PUBLISH WITH PRINT-ON-DEMAND (POD)

If you want to sell your self-published book, but you don't want to be in the business of storing and mailing your books, print-on-demand may be for you. Here's how it works: You sign a contract that gives an on-demand publisher the rights to print your book and distribute it on a book-by-book basis. The POD company retains control of your manuscript and will print the books as demand requires. These firms take orders for your book that are submitted by customers through your website or an online bookseller. Then the POD company will print copies of the book as they are purchased and mail them to customers.

Among the largest Print-On-Demand publishing companies are CreateSpace, iUniverse, and Lightning Source. CreateSpace, owned by Amazon, will give you a discount package for selling your book on Amazon and using their print-on-demand services. Some online publishers require the author to pay for a set number of printed books upfront, while others do not charge at the beginning, but instead keep a larger share of the sales and pay a royalty to the author. I suggest you research a variety of online printing companies to find the most attractive package that meets your publishing needs.

CREATE AN E-BOOK

While you are arranging for your book to be printed, you may want to have your manuscript formatted as an eBook too. An electronic book is published without printing any copies. It can be read on an electronic reader such as a Kindle or an iPad. You will need to hire a professional or use an online ePub site like Smashwords to convert your manuscript to an html (hypertext markup language) document that can be read on an electronic device. As these devices multiply and improve, more and more people enjoy reading books electronically.

PUBLISH YOUR BOOK ON A WEBSITE

Create a website or hire someone do it for you. Then post your memoir on the site. You can make the whole book available for free or you can charge a small fee to download the book or each chapter. Look on the Internet for companies to help you with your website project.

PRINT AND GIVE YOUR BOOK TO OTHERS

ASSEMBLE BOOK AT A COPY STORE

This is the easiest and least expensive way to create a book that you want to give away. First, design and lay out your book on your word processor or hire someone to do it for you. Then take your typewritten pages to a copy store and have them copied and spiral bound into an 8 ½" X 11" book. If you plan to add photos, you can group them on separate pages or add the photos to the manuscript pages. Many copy shops offer layout and design services for a fee or can recommend someone to help you.

Your copy shop should have a selection of thick papers in a variety of colors and textures that you can use for a cover. Have them print your book title, your name, and perhaps a photo on this thick stock to create a cover. You also can use an online cover-design program to create a professional-looking cover and then have the copy shop print the covers for your book.

Decide how many books you want to print. The shop personnel will print the number of copies you want and bind the book. Most copy shops do not have the equipment to do a "Perfect binding," such as you would find on professional-ly printed books. Instead they offer spiral or coil bindings, which come in a variety of widths and colors.

Self-Publish with an Online Company

As described above, self-publishing with an online com-pany will quickly produce a professional-looking book. You can choose to create a hard-cover or soft-cover book, with a Perfect binding and a cover design that you select. Companies such as Blurb and Lulu provide you with downloadable layout software that is easy and intuitive to use. Drag and drop your photos into place amid the text as you design your pages on the computer screen. The quality of the color reproductions and page stock used for these online books is outstanding.

Your biggest decisions will be how much you want to spend and how many books you want to have printed. They will be mailed to you all at once so that you can distribute them.

HIRE A LOCAL PRINTING COMPANY TO PRINT YOUR BOOK

There may be a small printing company in your community that can create hard- or soft-cover books with a Perfect binding. These printing companies may provide or recommend a book designer too, so you won't have to lay out the book yourself online. A book designer will reformat your typed pages to fit the size of the book you want, such as the common 6" x 9" or 5" x 8" sizes. The designer will resize and place photos among the text on pages where you want them, or group them on separate pages, depending on your wishes. Then you will receive a rough copy of the book to edit. The advantage of using a local printer is that you can work with a professional in person. Once you have given your final approval, the company will print the number of copies you want, say 100 to 200, and send them to you to distribute. The more books you order, the lower the cost per book.

CREATE A VIDEO MEMOIR

Have someone help you create an oral history of your life by making a video. You can read from your manuscript or answer planned questions. When you are finished, burn the video onto a DVD and give it to your family and friends. You may want to create a video in addition to your written memoir.

TIPS

❑ Lay out your book with text, photos, and other materials before you decide how you want to print it. Or hire a book designer to help make those final decisions.

❑ Compare prices carefully among self-publishing companies, especially if you are using their extra services like editing, proofing and marketing.

❑ Give yourself a deadline when you want to complete the book. If you want to give it to friends or family members in person, consider completing it for an upcoming anniversary or a holiday.

❑ Think about other people or institutions that should receive a copy of your memoir: libraries, professional colleagues, business associates, organizations, or universities.

You owe it to yourself to complete your memoir project by printing or publishing your book. You have come so far, following step-by-step to gather your ideas and then write and revise your manuscript.

Take the time now to decide how you want to print and/or publish your memoir. Put your best foot forward one more time as you take this last step.

FINAL WORDS

When you complete your book, you will feel a great sense of personal satisfaction. Few people are members of the Memoir Author's Club, although many desire to join. You have taken the time and made the effort to create a memoir that will become more valuable as time passes. You will be leaving behind a powerful and thoughtful written legacy.

Drop me a line at my email address: kayksanger@gmail.com. Tell me about your experience with memoir writing. I hope the 10 steps have helped you accomplish your goal. I am sincerely interested, because that is my reward for writing this book.

Now it's time for you to go out and live for today. You have finished examining your past. You have told your story. And in doing so, you have readied yourself to accept and understand new adventures in your future. I salute you and wish you all the best.

Suggested Readings

THIS SHORT LIST OF BOOKS about writing and memoir represents only a fraction of the creative works available on the subject. Each of these suggested readings will inspire you. An Internet search will turn up many more fine books. Make time to read while you write and learn as you go, to create your own memoir magic.

About Writing

Bradbury, Ray. *Zen in the Art of Writing.* New York: Bantam Books, 1992.

Dillard, Annie. *The Writing Life.* New York: Harper Perennial, 1998.

Goldberg, Natalie. *Writing Down the Bones: Freeing the Writer Within.* Boston and London: Shambhala, 1986.

Gornick, Vivian. *The Situation and the Story: The Art of Personal Narrative.* New York: Farrar, Straus & Giroux, 2001.

King, Stephen. *On Writing: A Memoir of the Craft.* New York: Scribner. 2000.

Lamott, Anne. *Bird by Bird, Some Instructions on Writing and Life.* New York: Pantheon Books, 1994.

Larson, Thomas. *The Memoir and the Memoirist: Reading and Writing Personal Narrative.* Athens, OH: Swallow Press/Ohio University Press, 2007.

Myers, Linda Joy. *The Power of Memoir. How to Write your Healing Story.* San Francisco: Jossey-Bass, 2010.

Miller, Brenda and Paola, Suzanne. *Tell It Slant: Creating, Refining and Publishing Creative Nonfiction.* Second Edition. New York: McGraw-Hill, 2012.

Norton, Lisa Dale. *Shimmering Images: A Handy Little Guide to Writing Memoir.* New York: St. Martin's Griffin, 2008.

Pennebaker, James W., and Janel D. Seagal. "Forming a Story: The Health Benefits of Narrative." *Journal of Clinical Psychology,* (1999) Vol. 55 (10), 1243-1254.

Reeves, Judy. *A Writer's Book of Days, A Spirited Companion and Lively Muse for the Writing Life.* Novato, CA: New World Library, 1999.

Zinsser, William K. *Inventing the Truth: The Art and Craft of Memoir.* Rev. Sub ed. Boston: Mariner Books, 1998.

MEMOIRS

Angelou, Maya. *I Know Why the Caged Bird Sings.* New York: Random House, 1970.

Child, Julia. *My Life in France.* New York: Alfred A. Knopf, 2006.

Conway, Jill Ker. *The Road from Coorain.* New York: Alfred A. Knopf, 1989.

Didion, Joan. *The Year of Magical Thinking.* New York: Vintage Books, 2007.

Dillard, Annie. *An American Childhood.* New York: Harper & Row, 1987.

Fey, Tina. *Bossypants.* New York: Reagan Arthur Books, 2011.

Gilbert, Elizabeth. *Eat, Pray, Love.* New York: Penguin, 2006.

Janzen, Rhoda. *Mennonite in a Little Black Dress: A Memoir of Going Home.* New York: Henry Holt and Company, 2009.

Jong, Erica. *Fear of Fifty.* New York: HarperCollins, 1994.

Karr, Mary. *The Liars' Club: A Memoir.* New York: Penguin Books, 1995.

McCourt, Frank. *Angela's Ashes: A Memoir.* New York: Scribner, 1996.

Nafisi, Azar. *Reading Lolita in Tehran.* New York: Random House, 2003.

Strayed, Cheryl. *Wild: From Lost to Found on the Pacific Crest Trail.* Alfred A. Knopf, 2011.

Trillin, Calvin. *Messages from My Father: A Memoir.* New York: Farrar, Straus & Giroux, 1996.

Welty, Eudora. *One Writer's Beginnings.* Cambridge, MA: Harvard University Press, 1984.

SUGGESTED READINGS

ABOUT THE AUTHOR

Kay Sanger is a writer and teacher who has authored seven books, including *Easter Island: The Essential Guide, Southern California for Kids, When the Animals were People* and *Discovering Prehistoric Rock Art*. During a 30-year career as a freelance writer, she has written magazine and newspaper articles for such publications as *Westways, Better Homes and Gardens, Meetings & Conventions*, the *Washington Post* and the *Los Angeles Times*.

Kay holds Masters degrees in education and archaeology. She teaches writing classes and facilitates memoir writing groups in Southern California, where she lives with her husband, author Tom Sanger.

CPSIA information can be obtained
at www.ICGtesting.com
Printed in the USA
FSHW020506200121
77827FS

9 780989 199001